Unhang
YOUR
HARP

Also by Ted Shuttlesworth Jr.

Blood on the Door: The Protective Power of Covenant

Blood on the Door: Workbook

*Praise. Laugh. Repeat: Living in the Power
of Overwhelming Joy*

*Praise. Laugh. Repeat. Devotional:
A 40-Day Journey to Overwhelming Joy*

Unhang YOUR HARP

HOW PRAISE OPENS THE DOOR TO EVERY BLESSING GOD HAS PROVIDED FOR YOU

TED SHUTTLESWORTH JR.

MIRACLE WORD
P U B L I S H I N G

Published in Virginia Beach, Virginia by Miracle Word Publishing.

Miracle Word titles may be purchased in bulk for educational, business, fundraising, or sales promotional use. For information, please e-mail info@miracleword.com

Unless otherwise indicated, all Scripture quotations are taken from the Holy Bible, New Living Translation, copyright © 1996, 2004, 2007, 2013 by Tyndale House Foundation. Used by permission of Tyndale House Publishers, Inc., Carol Stream, Illinois 60188. All rights reserved.

Scripture quotations are from the ESV® Bible (The Holy Bible, English Standard Version®), copyright © 2001 by Crossway, a publishing ministry of Good News Publishers. Used by permission. All rights reserved.

Scripture quotations marked KJV are from THE KING JAMES VERSION of the Bible, public domain.

Scripture quotations marked NKJV are from the NEW KING JAMES VERSION. © 1982 by Thomas Nelson, Inc. Used by permission. All rights reserved.

Scripture quotations marked NASB are taken from the New American Standard Bible®, Copyright © 1960, 1962, 1963, 1968, 1971, 1972, 1973, 1975, 1977, 1995 by The Lockman Foundation Used by permission." (www.Lockman.org)

Scripture quotations marked AMP are taken from the Amplified Bible, Copyright © 1954, 1958, 1962, 1964, 1965, 1987 by The Lockman Foundation. Used by permission.

Scripture quotations marked HCSB are taken from the Holman Christian Standard Bible®, Used by Permission HCSB ©1999,2000,2002,2003,2009 Holman Bible Publishers. Holman Christian Standard Bible®, Holman CSB®, and HCSB® are federally registered trademarks of Holman Bible Publishers.

All uppercase text in verses of scripture are added by the author for the purpose of emphasis.

ISBN 978-0-9909196-7-4

For Chris Vance and Lance Palmer
who both pushed me forward in praise.

Contents

— Part 2 —
Five Habits of a Dynamic Worshiper

Preface

"You're not a very good singer." That's the thought that resonated in my heart for over fifteen years.

I basically began leading worship out of necessity. After beginning to develop the gift to play the keyboard, my youth pastor asked me to start a band and lead worship in our youth group.

I felt extremely unprepared and unqualified. "I'll lead until someone who's good comes along and can take over," I told him.

The enemy used this premise in an attempt to hinder me for a long time. Whenever I was given the opportunity to lead worship (even on staff as a music director), the devil would whisper, "You're just a placeholder until someone good comes along."

I'd even tell people that I was a "keyboard player who sings" out of insecurity. Although I experienced some powerful times of worship, I felt stuck in my supposed inadequacy.

One Sunday, everything changed for me. I realized that if God had called me, He had qualified me. It was like I saw the vision of the children of Israel hanging their harps on the tree branches and being locked behind bars.

That would never be me.

Something melted away that morning and a freedom came to my worship. I no longer felt the stiffness of insecurity. I felt free. The power of my praise went to the next level and I didn't care what anyone thought of what I was producing for God.

As you read this book, I believe that you will not only gain a greater understanding of praise, but whatever the enemy is using to hinder your life or ministry will melt away as it did for me.

I pray that you experience a new level of power and manifestation in your life and ministry. If you're a worship leader, may this book bring you fresh revelation of your gift and encourage you to push for new levels.

The Weapon in The Willow Tree

Imagine spending seventy years in a prison with the key to your cell door laying on your window sill the entire time. You glance at it daily and shake your head. You weep as you think of your home and family, but you never pick up the key.

Seventy years is a lifetime. A lifetime without peace, joy, or freedom. The answer to your problems is staring you in the face, but you never make a move to retrieve it. Somehow your mind has been conditioned to believe that although you could take the key in your hands, it would do you no good.

This was the lie that God's children believed. Their problem was straightforward, but the solution eluded them for a lifetime.

God had promised Israel that if they would put Him first and worship Him only, He would bless them beyond measure. He promised that they would always be far above other nations (Deuteronomy 28:1).

In fact, God specifically told them that if they would faithfully praise and worship Him, He would conquer their enemies anytime they attacked.

However, God also gave them a warning. He described what would happen if their praise was ever misappropriated:

> *The Lord will exile you and your king to*
> *a nation unknown to you and your an-*
> *cestors. There in exile you will worship*
> *gods of wood and stone!*
> *Deuteronomy 28:36 NLT*

You'd think if God gave such clear, simple instructions, everyone would understand and comply.

You'd be wrong.

When the Israelites entered the Promised Land, they didn't obey God like they should have. God, however, was merciful. He gave them time to repent. For a few centuries, there was no king and instead of obeying God's instructions, everyone did what was right in his own eyes (Judges 21:25).

After this, Israel was ruled by their own kings. However, many of them didn't serve the Lord, and idolatry was rampant throughout the kingdom.

Although God sent His prophets to the people, they rebelled and most of the time would not listen to them.

Finally, during the reign of king Manasseh, the rebellion and idolatry reached its pinnacle. He erected altars to false gods, sacrificed his sons in the fire, and put an idol inside the temple in Jerusalem. (See 2 Kings 21:3-7.)

As a result, after years of mercy toward His people, God finally allowed them to be taken into captivity for seventy years — what could be considered a lifetime.

It's interesting to note that the same failure to praise and worship God — which put them in captivity — is the same failure that *kept* them in captivity.

Their praise, which had brought them victory so many times throughout their nation's history, was now thrown on the shelf. Their weapon was wasted:

> *By the rivers of Babylon, There we sat down and wept, when we remembered Zion. Upon the willows in the midst of it we hung our harps.*
>
> *Psalm 137:1-2 NASB*

They took their praise and worship — the very elements that God still desired — and cast them aside. Their lack of praise and worship placed them in bondage, and their failure to return to praise and worship kept them in bondage.

GET OUT OF THE WOODS

After over thirty years of serving the Lord and almost twenty years of ministering for Him, I have discovered for myself what many other powerful men and women of God have — the element that touches God's heart and pulls His presence into any situation.

It is this element that gives you leverage with the Divine Personality. This element hacks into Heaven's mainframe and inserts your name on God's personal calendar. It provokes divine intervention and shines a spotlight on you and your family when others remain in the darkness.

It is the element of *praise*.

That's why I'm encouraging you not only to take your weapon of praise off of the tree the enemy so conveniently placed by your previous failures or hurts, I'm encouraging you to praise your way out of the woods.

Don't let the devil mock you as your life remains devoid of Heaven's blessings. Praise your way into what

God has provided for you.

As you read this book, you'll discover how praise pulls divine healing into your body and how a calculated moment of praise brought feeling back into my father's legs. You'll see how a life of dedicated praise led one man to raise fourteen people (including his wife) from the dead.

I'll show you how praise transports you into extreme productivity and ensures that you'll never decrease. You'll see by revelation the secret the enemy uses to ensure you can't produce fruit in God's kingdom — and how to crush his plan.

One of the most interesting avenues we'll explore is how praise engenders supernatural unity which, when activated, makes the impossible possible. This is a principle so dynamic that God Himself has used division and confusion many times throughout history to ensure that His enemies didn't succeed. You'll read how a spirit of unity through praise caused a man's deaf ears to open instantly even though hands were never laid on him.

You will clearly see that praise is one of the ingredients God uses to bring financial prosperity and blessing into your life. You'll discover a secret that the Apostle Paul learned through deep study which keeps the enemy from destroying your financial harvests before they can be reaped.

In the second part of this book, I'll cover the five habits of a dynamic worshiper. I want to show you how you can transform cold, stagnant, worship into engaging, burden-lifting praise.

You will learn what is required to ensure that you carry the power of God's presence wherever you go so that you don't have to wait until you get to church to be refreshed.

Furthermore, you will be able to successfully develop the gift God has placed in your life. As you do, the Bible tells us that doors will open for you and you will be promoted by the One who gave you the gifts.

As you read this book, take time to stop and praise God. Worship Him and thank Him for His mighty Word and Spirit.

Don't allow yourself to remain frustrated as different aspects of God's promises are missing from your life. Engage in spiritual, scriptural praise, and watch as God opens the windows of Heaven over your family.

ONE

Praise Provokes Divine Healing

It was the final night of West Virginia Campmeeting—an annual spring revival hosted by my father—and we were in the middle of praising God.

The B3 Hammond organ was screaming in true Pentecostal fashion as we sang one of my favorite songs: *Funeral Plans.* You might think that's an odd name for a praise and worship song, but the lyrics are powerful.

When I die, let me die speaking in tongues . . .

People were shouting, clapping, and dancing as the atmosphere of faith and Holy Ghost power filled the church.

Something began to happen as we continued to praise God that night. All of a sudden, a man began to shout and took off running around the church.

Although his legs had been crippled for some time, as we were praising God and singing, the Holy Spirit touched him and he was instantly healed.

Just in front of him stood a man who was deaf in one ear and blind in one eye due to the effects of a previous surgery.

At the same moment the crippled man's legs were healed, this man's deaf ear began to hear and his blind eye opened.

Notice that no one laid hands on these men. The message hadn't even been preached yet. Healing was released simply by praising God.

PRAISE IS A FUNCTION OF LOVE

Hundreds of times throughout Scripture, believers are commanded to praise and worship the Lord. Praise and worship are one of the core functions of every believer.

Paul wrote that we were created *for* God (Colossians 1:16). God created us for Himself and then commanded us to praise Him.

Have you ever considered the fact that the reason God commanded us not to have any other gods before Him is because to praise other gods would be a direct departure from our intended purpose?

For God's children to praise and worship other gods (or even other things in life) would be just as out of place as hiring a plumber to work on your car or scheduling a surgery with your landscaping company. It's not their purpose and it would always end horribly.

In fact, any time God's children directed their praise and worship elsewhere throughout Scripture, it always ended in disaster.

This is not because God has a big ego; it's because praise is one of the main ways that He interacts with His children—which He desires to do.

Praise causes Jesus to reveal Himself to us. Jesus taught this concept to His disciples:

> *Those who accept my commandments and obey them are the ones who love me. And because they love me, my Father will love them. And I will love them and reveal myself to each of them.*
>
> *John 14:21 NLT*

When we obey the command to praise God, it is proof that we truly love Him. Praise is a function of love. We always praise what we love.

If you've never heard of Yelp, it's a website and app that allows anyone using it to find great local businesses and restaurants based upon the ratings and comments written by Yelp's community of users.

You can leave photos, videos, tips, and most importantly write reviews of any business for others to see before trying it out themselves.

You would think that no one would take the time to sit down and write a review unless things went sideways and they got angry, right? Business is supposed to work smoothly and that's our expectation.

However, that's not the case. As of September 30th, 2017, 68% of Yelp's 142 million reviews are *positive*. The majority of people aren't slamming experiences they hated; they're praising experiences they *loved*.

This principle is consistent even on the level of our personal relationships.

In Gary Chapman's international best-selling book *The 5 Love Languages*, he writes that one of the main ways people receive and show love is through words of affirmation. That's really just a fancy way of saying *praise*.

It's interesting to note that the reason we feel loved when we receive words of affirmation, is because we are created in the image of God Himself (Genesis 1:26). God is motivated by praise. Likewise, His children, who are created to be just like Him, are also motivated by praise.

However, praise that originates from love for God is

only the beginning of what Jesus taught in John chapter 14. He finished by saying that our obedience would result in the demonstration of His power as He reveals Himself to us.

Other translations use the word *manifest*. When we praise the Lord, Jesus will manifest Himself to us. Interestingly, that word means *to display by demonstration*.

It's vital to understand that Jesus won't just give you *knowledge* about Who He is, He will *do something* to show you who He is.

PRAISE GENERATES DIVINE DEMONSTRATION

As we've established, praise transports you into the presence of God where you'll find fullness of joy (Psalm 22:3; 16:11). Here, we take it a step further. Let's look at Psalm 16 again.

> *You make known to me the path of life;*
> *in your presence there is fullness of joy;*
> *at your right hand are pleasures forever-*
> *more.*
>
> *Psalm 16:11 ESV*

Overflowing joy is the initial blessing found in the presence of God, but we are also afforded the pleasures that are found at His right hand.

The word *pleasures* is translated from the Hebrew word *naiym* and literally means things that are delightful and sweet.

No doubt this is what David had in mind when he encouraged us to "taste and see that the Lord is good" (Psalm 34:8).

David begins Psalm 34 by declaring that he would continually praise the Lord. He then encourages us to join him in continual praise.

Knowing that the human mind is motivated to action by the possibility of personal benefit, David begins to list all of the supernatural perks of praise. Verse 10 is of interest to us for the purpose of this chapter:

> *The young lions suffer want and hunger; but those who seek the Lord lack NO GOOD THING.*
> *Psalm 34:10 ESV (Emphasis added)*

In context, David is saying that our praise provokes God to release to us every good thing He has in store.

Without a doubt, healing is one of the good things God has in store for us. We know this because healing is the bread that God gives His children as a gift. (See Matthew 15:21-28.) Furthermore, God only gives good gifts to His children (Matthew 7:11; James 1:17).

Praise can open the door to your healing very quickly. This was true of a blind man in the New Testament.

Bartimaeus, a blind beggar, was sitting on the side of the Jericho road as Jesus and His disciples were leaving the city with a large crowd following them.

Bartimaeus heard people in the crowd saying that Jesus of Nazareth was passing through the crowd.

It's interesting that these people referred to Him as Jesus of Nazareth as that was His *earthly* name. We have no record in Mark chapter 10 that Jesus stopped to bless anyone else in the crowd. Could this be because they were viewing Him as a mere man and not the Son of God?

We know that when Jesus returned to His hometown with the intention of producing miracles for those in need, He couldn't perform any mighty works because of their doubt. *They doubted His divinity!* (Mark 6:1-6.)

The same thing seems to be happening here. As Christ passes through, they seem to verbally disregard His divinity as the people of Nazareth did.

However, Bartimaeus, a man who could not see, saw more about the identity of Jesus than the entire crowd of people looking at Him with natural eyes.

> *. . . he began to cry out and say, "Jesus,*
> *Son of David, have mercy on me!"*
>
> *Mark 10:47 ESV*

Son of David was Jesus' Messianic name. Essentially, Bartimaeus was shouting, "Jesus! I believe you are the Messiah! Come and heal me because I know You can."

Just by simply saying this, Bartimaeus was praising Jesus. He was calling Him Savior, Deliverer, Healer, and the Anointed One. Look at the response of Christ:

> *And Jesus stopped and said, "Call him."*
>
> *Mark 10:49 ESV*

Regardless of what pressing matters Jesus may have had elsewhere, when Bartimaeus began praising Him, He could not have ignored Him. He had to manifest Himself to Bartimaeus by demonstrating His power.

Bartimaeus is a living example of God inhabiting our praise. The moment he began praising, Jesus called for him to come stand in His presence.

Jesus finished by giving Bartimaeus access to the pleasures that are at His right hand, and he was instantly healed.

It's important to note that when this story took place, Jesus wasn't in the middle of ministering. He wasn't preaching, teaching, or healing the sick. Jesus was *leaving town.*

Furthermore, Jesus didn't even know that Bartimaeus was in the crowd. It was Bartimaeus' praise that arrested Jesus' attention and provoked His power.

Quite literally, Bartimaeus penciled in his own miracle on Heaven's calendar through the avenue of praise.

This is possible for any of God's children. As Smith Wigglesworth, the famous British evangelist, famously said, "If the Spirit doesn't move me, I'll move Him."

PRAISE DESTROYS
THE ENEMY'S PLAN

I rolled over in bed and I glanced at my alarm clock. It was Easter Sunday morning and it was time to get ready for church. I winced as I sat up and threw the covers off.

Sharp pain shot through my head from a migraine headache and I felt completely nauseous. My joints ached as I made my way to the shower.

Although I wanted to crawl back into bed, I couldn't. I was the praise and worship leader for our church. Countless times I had encouraged my team to put God first and be faithful no matter what they were going through (effectively painting myself into a corner).

I showered, put on my suit, and drove to church. When I arrived, the thundering sound of our pre-service band practice intensified my headache, and my stomach felt like it was about to give out.

I turned and warned my band and choir, "No matter what you see me do, keep praising God. I may run out of the church, I may bend over and vomit, but keep praising."

I took my position behind the keyboard and squinted out into the crowd as the band started our first song. We began to sing and play joyfully to God.

Something began to happen as we faithfully obeyed God's command to praise Him. First, the migraine left. Next, my joints stopped aching. Finally, all signs of nausea were gone.

Before the first song had come to an end, every flu-like symptom had left my body, and I was healed.

All through the Bible, it's plain to see that divine intervention is provoked by man's celebration.

SCHEDULE A SUPERNATURAL SURGERY

When people seek treatment or are taking medication for a particular sickness or disease, it's always done on a schedule. Many medications must be taken at particular times throughout the day and not be administered too close together.

Cancer patients who have chosen to take chemotherapy must schedule those sessions and receive them on the hospital's prescribed time line.

Have you ever considered creating a schedule of daily praise to facilitate your divine healing? Many times when people are faced with the difficulties of life, they begin to pray harder than ever before.

I'm not belittling the power of prayer. Prayer is one of the most important things we could ever do as believers. However, to pray without praising God is like loading a gun but never pulling the trigger.

As Bishop David Oyedepo wrote, "Although prayer has its place, it cannot compete with praise in potency."

Smith Wigglesworth, who was an evangelist from Bradford, England, saw the power of praise throughout his entire ministry.

During the time he ministered — from the late 1800s through the early 1900s — he raised fourteen people from the dead, including his own wife, Polly.

Those who knew him personally wrote that one of the main characteristics that set his life apart was his dedication to praising the Lord.

Every morning, Wigglesworth would wake up and

dance before the Lord for ten minutes while thanking God for giving him another day to serve Him.

He scheduled sessions in the presence of the Great Physician. You can do the same. Although no one feels like waking up and dancing or praising God, a dedication to praise will loose health and strength to your body afresh each day.

When you dedicate yourself to the presence of God privately, He will always reward you publicly. (See Matthew 6:6.)

In the late 1980s, the devil launched a severe attack against my father. After preaching crusades and seeing many miracles take place, he collapsed and was bedridden.

His heart was racing and the doctor gave him sedatives, but he could not feel his legs and it seemed as though the situation was getting worse.

At one point, he became so angry at the devil that he said, "I am going to get up out of this bed and dance before the Lord." He recounts the story in his own words in his book *How to Destroy the Works of a Buffeting Spirit:*

> Although my legs seemed dead, I took my hand and pulled them out of the bed and fell over against the window and grabbed hold. It seemed I heard the mocking voice of the

enemy but I said out loud, "I am dancing in the Spirit!" When I did, a tingling started in my legs. I began to shout and walk! I have been shouting and walking ever since!

Without a doubt, praise creates an atmosphere of miracles and healing. I want to encourage you to develop your own daily praise schedule.

As Smith Wigglesworth understood, dedication and consistency produce lasting results. It's not about trying it once or twice.

I often joke that it would be as ridiculous as going to the gym and working out once and then going home to look in the mirror and becoming upset when you find that you look exactly the same. You can't be discouraged. It's consistency that brings the change. I'll finish with David's encouragement to employ the power of consistent praise:

> *I will bless the Lord at ALL TIMES; his praise shall CONTINUALLY be in my mouth.*
> *Psalm 34:1 ESV (Emphasis added)*

GOD HAS GIVEN US A CURE FOR
THE SPIRIT OF HEAVINESS.
HIS PRESCRIPTION IS PRAISE.

#UnhangYourHarp

TWO

Praise Activates God's Word

♆♆♆♆♆

Years ago, during a revival my father was holding, a woman approached him to ask if he would pray for her husband. My father agreed to pray if she would bring him to the services.

The woman told my father that her husband was being attacked mentally and indicated that he needed supernatural deliverance.

When they returned and approached the altar, the woman's husband appeared to be on the verge of a nervous breakdown.

In an effort to get more information regarding his situation, my father asked the man how and when the attacks began.

At the time this story took place, the United States

was embroiled in the Persian Gulf War in the Middle East. Needless to say, every major news network provided plenty of coverage during this two-year period.

The man told my father that he had moved all three of his televisions into his living room, and turned each TV to a different news network that followed the Desert Storm conflict.

By his own admission, he stayed home most days and followed the coverage closely as his wife continued to bring him fresh cups of coffee.

His constant engagement with the turmoil of the world was destroying his peace and joy. Notice, this man and his wife were Christians and attended church. They already had Christ in their lives.

One might argue that he just needed more of God's Word in his life. While that may be true, that is definitely not the answer to this situation.

Do you realize that no matter how much or how little of God's Word this man had taken into his spirit, it would not work for him?

In fact, I'm about to show you a secret about praise and worship from God's Word that should highlight the importance of its purpose in your mind.

Even though God's Word is the most powerful force in the universe—containing even more power than the name of God (see Psalm 138:2)—there are things that can render its power useless.

In Mark chapter 4, Jesus taught His disciples the parable of the sower. Jesus indicated that this parable was so important, that the disciples' understanding of the rest of the parables that He would teach hinged on their understanding of this one story (Mark 4:13).

In this parable, the sower sowed the Word of God and it fell upon four different types of ground: the wayside, rocky ground, thorny ground, and good ground.

Jesus then began to teach that each type of ground affects how the Word of God is received. For the purpose of this chapter, I only want to focus on one type of ground: *thorny ground.*

When Jesus finally explained the meaning of this story to His disciples, He revealed the effects that thorny ground would have when His Word was sown into someone's heart:

> *Now these are the ones sown among thorns; they are the ones who hear the word, and the CARES OF THIS WORLD, the deceitfulness of riches, and the desires for other things entering in choke the word, and it becomes UNFRUITFUL.*
> *Mark 4:18-19 NKJV (Emphasis added)*

The cares of this world. These are the negative reports that could be taken from the natural circumstances of life. When you receive the cares of this world into your heart instead of the truth of God's Word, it brings what the Bible calls a *spirit of heaviness.*

DEALING WITH A SPIRIT
OF HEAVINESS

It's vitally important that we understand a spirit of heaviness destroys the ability for God's Word to produce any kind of fruit in your life.

That blows the minds of most people I talk to. "God can do anything!" They boldly declare in response. I always answer with a question.

"Does God want anyone to go to hell?"

Most Christians have been in church long enough that they can recall the verse that says God is "not willing that any should perish, but that all should come to repentance" (2 Peter 3:9).

"Oh, no," they'll respond quoting a portion of the verse. "He's not willing that any should perish!"

"Will there be any people who perish?" That follow-up question usually leaves people very quiet as they search for a response.

The point I'm trying to make, is that although God doesn't *want* anyone to die eternally, there will be many who *do not* find the way to Heaven (Matthew 7:14).

To be very clear, God *cannot* do anything He wants to do. God's actions are limited to the confines of His written Word.

Part of the reason that people cannot see God's intervention in their lives, is because when the cares of this world are allowed to dominate your mind, it brings division to your thoughts.

On one hand, you know what God's Word says, on the other hand, however, you begin to place weight in what you've heard from an extra-biblical source.

This is called *double mindedness*. Look what the Bible says regarding that type of person:

> **. . . the one who doubts is like a wave of the sea that is driven and tossed by the wind. For that person must not suppose that he will receive anything from the Lord; he is a double-minded man, unstable in all his ways.**
>
> **James 1:6-8 ESV**

Now you can clearly see why the thorny ground produced by the cares of this world can so easily choke out God's ability to produce His blessings in your life through His Word.

It's because the cares of this world, if not placed in check, lead to doubt and double mindedness.

Thankfully, God has given us a cure for the spirit of heaviness. His prescription is *praise.*

> *"The Spirit of the Lord God is upon Me,*
> *Because the Lord has anointed Me . . .*
> *To give them beauty for ashes, The oil*
> *of joy for mourning, The GARMENT OF*
> *PRAISE for the spirit of heaviness . . ."*
> *Isaiah 61:1, 3 NKJV (Emphasis added)*

Notice that God has given us a garment of praise *for* the spirit of heaviness. That means this is a transaction or a trade off. You cannot wear both of these at the same time. You must take one off and put the other on.

The reason for this is that these two forces are polar opposites. One translation renders the word *heaviness* as *despair*, or the complete loss or absence of hope.

Where hope is absent, depression takes control. That is why these two forces are polar opposites. When you truly praise God, you are immediately transported into His presence (Psalm 22:3).

In fact, as Bishop David Oyedepo — pastor of the largest church in the world—has often taught, praise is the cheapest access into the presence of God.

When you're in God's presence, the Bible teaches that you have entered into the *fullness of joy.* (See Psalm 16:11.) You cannot stand in the fullness of joy and be shrouded by overwhelming despair and depression at the same time.

By transporting you into supernatural joy, praise completely destroys the spirit of heaviness in your life.

This is what allows God's Word to not only take root in your heart, but produce supernatural benefits in your life. We were not designed to carry a heavy load generated by anxiety and worry. Look at this verse:

> *Casting all your cares [all your anxieties, all your worries, and all your concerns, once and for all] on Him, for He cares about you [with deepest affection, and watches over you very carefully].*
> *1 Peter 5:7 AMP*

"Christianity is a hard life," some people will tell you. "But it will all be worth it one day when we get to Heaven." (This last part seems to make what they're saying more holy and true.)

This is completely contrary to what Jesus taught. Je-

sus described the benefits of those who would follow
Him in this way:

> *Come to Me, all you who labor and are*
> *heavy laden, and I will give you rest.*
> *Take My yoke upon you and learn from*
> *Me, for I am gentle and lowly in heart,*
> *and you will find rest for your souls. For*
> *My yoke is easy and My burden is light.*
> *Matthew 11:28-30 NKJV*

Praise produces a *rested soul*; heaviness produces a
tortured soul. I want you to understand that this is about
more than just how you feel. The joy and freedom that
come through praising God determine our ability to access the blessings that He has set aside for us.

THE PLANTING OF THE LORD

Let's revisit Isaiah chapter 61 for a moment. I want you
to see the other side of the coin. The enemy wants you to
become thorny ground, but God — through the avenue
of praise — transforms you into good ground.

> *To give them ... The garment of praise for*
> *the spirit of heaviness; That they may be*
> *called trees of righteousness, The plant-*
> *ing of the Lord, that He may be glorified.*
> *Isaiah 61:3 NKJV*

Notice Isaiah is saying that when the spirit of heaviness leaves your life, you become the *planting of the Lord* which will bring glory to God.

As the garment of praise is activated and the spirit of heaviness is cast away from your life, you'll begin to produce fruit at a rapid rate. Praise is one of the main elements that keeps you connected to Christ and keeps His words at work in you.

In the same way that God is attracted when you praise Him, His Word is also attracted. David understood this and wrote:

> *In God, whose word I praise, in the*
> *LORD, whose word I praise,*
> *Psalm 56:10 ESV*

Not only are you connected to Christ as you praise Him, you attract and are filled with His Word. This ensures that you will produce fruit at a high level, and you'll bring glory to God.

Not everyone is qualified to be the planting of the Lord. In fact, as I've shown you in this chapter, it's probably the thing the enemy fights the hardest in the life of every believer.

Satan doesn't want you to receive the revelation of God's Word and produce fruit with it. He doesn't want you to go to another level. He would rather keep you in the habit of attending church thinking you're moving forward when in reality he's choking out every revelation that comes your way.

Praise changes all of that. Jesus echoed Isaiah's thought in the New Testament. He told His disciples:

> *But if you remain in me and my words remain in you, you may ask for anything you want, and it will be granted! When you produce much fruit, you are my true disciples. This brings great glory to my Father.*
>
> *John 15:7-8 NLT*

This may be the most important chapter in this book because every part of our inheritance from God comes through His mighty Word. That's why the Apostle Paul wrote to the elders in Ephesus:

> *And now I commend you to God and to*
> *the word of his grace, which is able to*
> *build you up and to GIVE YOU THE IN-*
> *HERITANCE among all those who are*
> *sanctified.*
> *Acts 20:32 ESV (Emphasis added)*

Praise makes us dangerous. It ensures increase in every one of our lives. If the revelation of God's Word cannot be withheld from us, promotion and increase cannot be withheld either.

As I wrote at the beginning of the chapter, God is confined to the boundaries of His Word. Praising God on a daily basis opens your heart to abundant joy which activates the power of His Word in every area of your life. As you do, get ready to be refreshed and experience the divine intervention of God.

THE ENEMY SEEKS TO STEAL UNITY
SO THE IMPOSSIBLE NEVER
BECOMES POSSIBLE

#UnhangYourHarp

THREE

Praise Makes The Impossible Possible

I bent down and grabbed my Bible off of the chair behind me and walked from the front row of the church onto the platform. As I have done many times before, I sat down at the keyboard to lead a few more songs before I stood to preach that night's message.

I could feel faith and expectancy in my spirit as I began to play and sing. I chose a medley of old, campmeeting choruses. (In case you've never been to a Pentecostal campmeeting, these are hymns that have been sped up to about twice the normal tempo and sung at about three times the normal volume.)

I could feel the atmosphere change as it became infused with supernatural joy and faith. As always, I encouraged the congregation to clap their hands and sing loudly with me.

I do this because praise and worship are not meant to be a performance that is observed by the crowd. All too often, I see people during church services who are standing with their hands in their pockets, watching as the worship team leads from the platform.

Worship is not a concert. It's not meant to be viewed. God designed praise and worship as a time when His children would engage Him with open hearts.

I learned at a young age that when the congregation is completely engaged in praise and worship, it brings unity into a service.

Unity is a vital component. It is absolutely necessary if we are going to see God move miraculously in our church services. Notice that God's Spirit begins to move as unity is established.

> *When the Day of Pentecost had fully come, they were all with ONE AC-CORD in one place. And suddenly there came a sound from heaven, as of a rushing mighty wind, and it filled the whole house where they were sitting.*
> *Acts 2:1-2 NKJV (Emphasis added)*

We can clearly see that the Holy Spirit was not poured

out upon everyone who knew and followed Jesus. The Spirit was given to the 120 people who had obeyed the instructions of Christ by waiting in Jerusalem.

Their collective obedience to a single instruction brought them into unity. As a result, the power of God fell upon *all who were present in unity.*

Two chapters later, after being persecuted for doing the work Christ had assigned them, those same believers gathered in a house to pray.

They returned to those with whom they had unity. They understood that their spiritual power was activated by unity of purpose. After they had been persecuted and threatened, the Scripture says:

> *. . . they raised their voice to God with ONE ACCORD . . . And when they had prayed, the place where they were assembled together was shaken; and they were all filled with the Holy Spirit, and they spoke the word of God with boldness.*
>
> *Acts 4:24, 31 NKJV (Emphasis added)*

When God's children come together in unity, it activates supernatural power and makes the impossible possible.

King David understood that power. He wrote that when brothers dwell together in unity, it's good and pleasant. Then he added something very interesting— he wrote that unity carries the same power as the anointing God released to Aaron the Old-Testament priest.

David likened unity to the power of God in the mountains of Zion where God commands His blessing and gives life forevermore. (See Psalm 133:1-3.)

As David understood, and as we see modeled throughout the Bible, unity carries power and also makes the impossible possible.

In the Old Testament, we can see that the unity principle is true even in a negative context.

After the flood of Noah's time, people began to travel from the east to settle near Babylonia. These people did not fear or worship God. They had an idolatrous form of worship which was dedicated to many false gods.

They made up their minds that they would build a tower dedicated to the heavens with signs of the Zodiac portrayed as visible objects of worship.

God saw the wickedness of their hearts and said:

> *"Behold, they are one people, and they have all one language, and this is only the beginning of what they will do. And nothing that they propose to do will now*

> *be impossible for them. Come, let us go down and there confuse their language, so that they may not understand one an- other's speech."*
>
> **Genesis 11:6-7 ESV**

Did you see that? God Himself said that because they had total unity, nothing they decided to do would be impossible!

In order to cancel their evil plans, God had to bring division into their wicked unity.

This is also a function of unified praise and worship. God used His people's unity in praise throughout the Bible to bring confusion and division to their enemies.

In 2 Chronicles chapter 20, three enemy armies united to fight against God's people. King Jehoshophat and the people of Judah and Jerusalem realized that they could not win this battle on their own. So they stood before the Lord in unity to receive an answer from Heaven (2 Chronicles 20:13).

The next morning, as God had instructed them, they went out against the three armies. The king appointed singers to go out ahead of Israel's army, and they all praised God in unity. Look at the result:

> *At the very moment they began to sing and give praise, the Lord caused the armies of Ammon, Moab, and Mount Seir to start fighting among themselves . . . So when the army of Judah arrived at the lookout point in the wilderness, all they saw were dead bodies lying on the ground as far as they could see. Not a single one of the enemy had escaped.*
>
> *2 Chronicles 20:22, 24 NLT*

God took their praise and worship and transformed it into confusion and division in the camp of their enemies. They didn't even have to fight as they praised the One Who always gives us the victory.

THE DESTRUCTION OF DIVISION

Division is always a precursor to destruction. That's why the devil fights so hard to bring division among God's people. He knows that if he can divide them, he can easily break them.

But unity ensures that you will experience strength and victory. Look how King Solomon described the power of unity:

> *A person standing alone can be attacked and defeated, but two can stand back-to-back and conquer. Three are even better, for a triple-braided cord is not easily broken.*
>
> *Ecclesiastes 4:12 NLT*

Pride is one of the tools the devil uses to divide God's people. Satan knows all too well how pride can destroy unity with God.

Pride entered into his heart when he was still one of God's angels. He made up his mind that he would be like the most-high God. He planned to ascend and take the throne (Isaiah 14:12-21).

Obviously, his plan was thwarted, but since other angels had already taken his side, Lucifer's pride caused a great division in Heaven as one-third of the angels were ejected with him. (See Revelation 12:3-9.)

Satan has been using pride to bring division since the beginning of time. It's interesting that pride is one of the main obstacles to freely praising God.

We worry about what people may think of us if we're truly uninhibited in our worship.

I'm too dignified to act like that. People know me here. I'm held in high regard in this community. What would people think of me if I acted that way?

These are thoughts the enemy would love for you to embrace. He wants you to think praise and worship is about *you*. However, praise and worship is truly about the *object* of our worship: God Almighty.

To be quite truthful, Christians really have no other option but to praise the Lord. We have no say in the matter. Throughout Scripture, we are commanded again and again to praise the Lord. As an example, read Psalm 150 which even lists the ways we're to praise God.

Worship is for God alone. It's about Him. He reaps our love and affection; we reap the benefits of His presence.

No matter how high you rise in life, you're never too dignified to give the Lord enthusiastic praise and worship.

When David had become the king of Israel, his first order of business was to recover the Ark of the Covenant and bring the anointing back to Jerusalem.

When he and his elite soldiers had retrieved it, they came back toward the entrance of the city engaged in enthusiastic praise.

> *And David danced before the Lord with all his might, wearing a priestly garment. So David and all the people of Israel brought up the Ark of the Lord with*

> *shouts of joy and the blowing of rams'*
> *horns.*
>
> *2 Samuel 6:14-15 NLT*

Although David was king, he acted as the priest and led the people in unified praise and worship. As a result, he ushered the presence and power of God back into Jerusalem.

Notice the unity that was ignited through David's humility. As the king, he could have assigned someone else go out with the Ark and praise God on his behalf. He could have formed a worship team to usher it in with a formal procession while he sat regally on his throne.

However, that kind of attitude is not why God labeled David a man after His own heart (Acts 13:22).

David understood that personal and corporate praise and worship were the prerequisites for God's supernatural favor. He was not ashamed to give God all of his strength in praise.

But not everyone in the kingdom of Israel shared King David's enthusiasm.

> *. . . Michal, the daughter of Saul, looked*
> *down from her window. When she saw*
> *King David leaping and dancing before*
> *the Lord, she was filled with contempt*

> *for him . . . So Michal, the daughter of Saul, remained childless throughout her entire life.*
>
> **2 Samuel 6:16, 23 NLT**

I want to draw your attention to something interesting in this passage. Michal was David's wife, but in 2 Samuel 6, the Bible refers to her three times as *Saul's daughter.*

Saul also had great contempt for David. What the Bible is telling us here is that although Michal was joined to David in marriage, she didn't share a common spirit with David. She had the spirit of her father, Saul.

It was a wonderful thing that the Ark of the Covenant was coming back to Israel. It meant that order, authority, victory, and provision were coming back to the nation. As a citizen of Israel, Michal had just as much reason to praise God as her husband, David.

Pride gripped Michal's heart and what should have been rejoicing became revulsion. God made sure that we saw the result of her attitude before the chapter came to an end: she remained childless throughout her life.

The absence of praise always leads to the absence of production. We can see a contrast in David's story. His lifestyle of praise caused him to continue in forceful production for God throughout the rest of his days.

Extreme praise opens the door for extreme production. This is a concept we will explore in depth later on.

Pride brought division into David's own home. If the enemy can rob us of unity, he can remove the ability to make the impossible possible.

Pride is the door that admits every evil work and attack of the enemy into your life. The Bible tells us that true wisdom is shown by its works of *meekness* (James 3:13). Another word for meekness is *humility*.

When pride is allowed to take control of someone's personality, they're exhibiting the nature of Satan. However, when meekness and humility are shown throughout their life, they're displaying the nature of Christ (Matthew 11:29).

It's important to insert here that meekness is the key to greatness and inheritance. True meekness brings a person into unity with God's Word. Jesus taught:

> *"Blessed are the meek, for they shall inherit the earth."*
> *Matthew 5:5 ESV*

This was true for Moses. The Bible reveals that he was the meekest man in all of the earth (Numbers 12:3). Another passage tells us that Moses had become very great in the land of Egypt (Exodus 11:3). His extreme meekness brought about extreme greatness.

Pride goes before destruction, but humility goes before promotion.

James shows us the result if meekness is absent and pride has taken control:

> *For where envy and self-seeking exist,*
> *confusion and EVERY EVIL THING are*
> *there.*
> *James 3:16 NKJV (Emphasis added)*

What an eye-opening verse. Pride is a magnet that draws every evil thing into your life. No wonder the devil fights so hard to insert pride, confusion, and division into the body of Christ.

We can now see why division and strife are such demonic elements. The Apostle Paul dealt with them harshly in the churches he planted. He knew the destructive effects that would follow division. For that reason, he treated division like a surgeon treats a cancerous tumor. He surgically removed it.

> *As for a person who stirs up division,*
> *after warning him once and then twice,*
> *have nothing more to do with him,*
> *Titus 3:10 ESV*

This may seem harsh to those who have never seen this before. It may seem as though Paul the Apostle is not exhibiting "grace" or "walking in love" toward these kinds of people. On the contrary, he is showing love to the rest of the body by removing the cancerous spirit of division from among those who have not yet been contaminated.

In the time that I have been leading praise and worship (almost 20 years at the time of this writing), I've noticed the element that suppresses the true spirit of praise and worship more than any other is offense caused by pride and division.

This is a slimy trick of the enemy to stifle our unity in praise, which is the supernatural element that makes the impossible possible.

We've all seen these situations. Sister Easily Offended with her arms folded and staring daggers across the auditorium at Sister Facebook Post. The next thing you know, Sister Easily Offended's whole family is mad at Sister Facebook Post and her family.

Now there's a total division in the church. Now bitterness and anger occupy the place where there used to be a sweet spirit of praise and worship, and the impossible . . . remains impossible.

LET'S GO BACK TO THE BEGINNING

Don't worry. I didn't forget the story I started the chapter with. We're back to the revival meeting, and I'm sitting behind the keyboard playing and singing as joy and unity filled the room.

While singing, I could see some of the older saints smile as they were transported back to a time when these old campmeeting choruses were the standard practice for many services.

The Lord had instructed me to minister on healing when I preached that night.

At the end of the service, I encouraged anyone who needed healing to join me at the altar where I would lay hands on them and pray for a miracle to take place.

When I was almost finished praying for those who had filled the altar that night, I came to an elderly man with a big smile on his face.

"What do you need God to do for you?" I asked him.

"Well, brother, I came to church tonight believing for God to open my ears and I was going to have you pray for me. But tonight, at the beginning of the service, when you were singing the second song, my ears immediately came open," he said with a laugh.

I never even got a chance to pray for him. As we praised and worshiped God in perfect unity, the power of God's Spirit came into the room, and the impossible was made possible.

THE WORSHIP OF JOYFUL GIVING
ENSURES YOUR HARVEST WILL
NEVER WITHER

#UnhangYourHarp

FOUR

Praise Unlocks Financial Prosperity

Imagine a man who is lost in a desert. He's been stranded for almost forty-eight hours with no water. Parched and tired, he wanders through the sand hoping to find civilization before he dies of dehydration.

To his relief, he finally sees a small town in the distance. With his remaining strength, he scurries across the sand and into the small oasis of the town.

At the point of collapse, he arrives at the town's well. Finally, fresh water that will give him new life is within his grasp.

He stumbles over to it, falls to his knees to draw from the well and drink the cool, clean water only to find that the well has no bucket.

He can see the water at the bottom of the well, but

it's out of his natural reach. If he only had a bucket and rope, he could draw this refreshing substance from the well.

This is the story of many Christians today. It's also one of the reasons that the enemy employs a spirit of heaviness against us.

As long as he can keep us devoid of supernatural joy, we have no ability to access the refreshing water of salvation. Look at what the Prophet Isaiah wrote:

> **With joy you will draw water from the wells of salvation.**
> **Isaiah 12:3 ESV**

Notice that *joy* is the bucket that allows us to draw water from the wells of salvation.

Many people incorrectly assume that salvation is just freedom from eternal damnation. While this is the greatest achievement of the salvation that Christ purchased for us, it is definitely not the only benefit.

In the New Testament, one of the words that we translate as *salvation* in English is the Greek word *sozo*.

This is important to mention here because *sozo* gives much more depth to the word salvation. It encompasses several things.

Some of the benefits include rescue from danger or

destruction, safety from injury or peril, or salvation of a suffering one from disease by healing, making well, and restoring to health.

The benefits of salvation are numerous. Jesus won an amazing victory through His redemptive act. Let me direct your attention to one verse of Scripture that will give you a glimpse into the depth of what's available to the believer through their salvation covenant:

> *"Worthy is the Lamb that was slain to receive power and riches and wisdom and might and honor and glory and blessing."*
>
> *Revelation 5:12 NASB*

Just these seven redemptive benefits encompass every area of a believer's life. You receive might (or strength) physically, wisdom mentally, riches and blessing financially, power and glory spiritually, and honor generationally.

It's interesting to note that the Greek word translated honor is *timê* (pronounced tee-may). This word actually means to restore value by giving a precious price.

Literally, your redemption has made you a valuable entity. You are no longer a liability to your generation; you are an asset because the blessing of Abraham has been transferred to you through Christ. You are no longer a nobody; you've become a valued, high-ranking official in the Kingdom of God:

> *Through Christ Jesus, God has blessed the Gentiles with the same blessing he promised to Abraham, so that we who are believers might receive the promised Holy Spirit through faith.*
>
> *Galatians 3:14 NLT*

Without question, the enemy doesn't want you to receive these earthly blessings. So what does he do? He doesn't have the power to stop you from receiving them. Jesus stripped him of all power (Colossians 2:15).

Instead, he tries to steal your praise and joy. The devil wants you to be the one wandering through life . . . a life that he has made a desert by robbing you of refreshing. He doesn't mind if you have a well as long as you don't have a bucket.

PRAISE KEEPS YOUR HARVEST RIPE

Joyful giving is a form of praise and worship. Once we understand the full transaction God expects to make with us, we can see what giving really is.

When God created the system of "seedtime and harvest," He was creating a two-sided system. He promised that no matter what happened in the future, nothing would abolish seedtime and harvest (Genesis 8:22).

Through improper teaching or mere ignorance to what God intended, some people only view giving as seedtime. As a result, they expect no return when they give. They do it as though they're giving a donation to the church. We don't give donations; we sow seeds. There is a big difference between the two.

To be clear, God doesn't need donations. He sits on a throne. Underneath His feet are streets of pure gold and the gates of His city are made from one pearl. Heaven is opulent.

Seedtime and harvest are a system that God established to bless His people. Paul wrote:

> *Do not be deceived, God is not mocked; for whatever a man sows, this he will also reap.*
>
> *Galatians 6:7 NASB*

Notice that Paul is saying God's system of sowing and reaping will not be mocked. God will ensure that whatever someone sows (in accordance with God's instruction on how to sow) they will reap.

But did you know there is a way to sow seeds to God but it not be praise or worship? There's a way to give that ensures nothing will come back to you as a result.

The enemy wants to steal the praise aspect from your giving so that there's no return.

When Paul was giving the Corinthian church instructions on giving, he wrote something that will open our eyes to God's way of giving.

> *. . . don't give reluctantly or in response to pressure. "For God loves a person who gives cheerfully."*
>
> *2 Corinthians 9:7 NLT*

The reason the final part of this verse is in quotes is because the Apostle Paul is quoting another verse from the Bible as he is teaching the Corinthians. The verse he's quoting is found in the Greek version of Proverbs 22:8 which includes an additional proverb:

> *God blesses a man who gives cheerfully, but his worthless deeds will come to an end.*
>
> *Proverbs 22:8 LXX (Greek Septuagint)*

In context, Paul is teaching the Corinthians that when you give reluctantly or without joy in your heart, your giving becomes a worthless deed.

Worthless deeds come to an end while God's system of sowing an reaping has no end. Do you see it? As you sow cheerfully, it ensures that God will bless your seed. God doesn't bless seeds that aren't sown joyfully, which is why Paul is warning the Corinthian believers.

The enemy knows what happens to your harvest when joy is removed from your giving:

> *. . . The harvest of the field is perished. The vine is dried up, and the fig tree languisheth; the pomegranate tree, the palm tree also, and the apple tree, even all the trees of the field, are withered: BECAUSE JOY IS WITHERED AWAY from the sons of men.*
>
> *Joel 1:11-12 KJV (Emphasis added)*

The enemy can cause your harvest to wither and die in the field before you ever have a chance to reap it if he can steal your ability to sow your seeds with a joyful heart.

Conversely, when you enter into God's system and method of sowing and reaping, the enemy has no ability to touch your harvest. Once again, joy allows you to draw water from the wells of your salvation.

God specifically outlined what He would do for His children when they obeyed His command to tithe and give from a willing and joyful heart.

He said that He would personally rebuke the devil when he comes to devour our harvest in the field. (See Malachi 3:8-12.)

This is one of the main reasons that praise is such a vital component in the life of a believer. Any blessing from God's Word can only be received through the receptacle of joy. Joy is a direct result of a life of praise to God.

PRAISE AND THE
PROPHETIC ANOINTING

Did you know that everything God does on the earth is released through the prophetic anointing? In fact, God *will not* do anything unless that prophetic anointing is provoked. Look at what the prophet Amos wrote:

> *For the Lord God does nothing without revealing his secret to his servants the prophets.*
>
> *Amos 3:7 ESV*

Even Jesus could not come to the earth as the Messiah until hundreds of prophecies were given describing his birth, life, ministry, and death. When God's prophetic word goes forth, it always produces prosperous results. God spoke through the prophet Isaiah and described the function of His Word:

> *So shall My word be that goes forth from My mouth; It shall not return to Me void, But it shall accomplish what I please, And IT SHALL PROSPER in the thing for which I sent it.*
> *Isaiah 55:11 NKJV (Emphasis added)*

God's Word always prospers. God works this way because His Word is the avenue through which He creates. He speaks things into being.

Did you know that something as simple as the path of the earth's orbit and distance from the sun is so fragile that if it were to go off course or change it's timing, it could destroy our seasons, harvests of crops, coastal cities and much more?

That cannot happen, however, because Christ upholds the universe by His Word. (See Hebrews 1:3 ESV.)

It's so important to understand that God's Prophetic Word is required for any type of supernatural increase.

Without it, we are forced to depend on the natural sources of provision and prosperity.

PROVISION LIKE A FLOOD

I had just started a revival in northeast Pennsylvania. I came to the church Sunday night with a powerful message on deliverance in my heart. I was ready to unload it and believe for miracles to flow from Heaven.

However, something happened as we finished praising God. I took the microphone and began to exhort, but I wasn't talking about deliverance. I wasn't even going in the direction of the message I had prepared that night. I knew the Holy Spirit was leading us somewhere.

I began to preach on financial prosperity. As I was preaching, I turned to the Pastor and began to prophesy.

"Expedited increase is getting ready to come to this church," I said. I hadn't planned on saying that. In fact, as I was saying it, my natural mind wanted to push the prophecy further out into the future.

I thought to myself, *If something doesn't quickly happen financially, you'll look like a fool, or worse, a false prophet!*

That was the enemy trying to insert those thoughts in my mind. Any time you begin to speak faith, he will attempt to pull you into a spirit of fear.

The Pastor raised his hand in agreement and received the word from the Lord. The church was building an amphitheater for outreach events which would be one of the largest venues in the region.

As that revival came to an end, powerful testimonies immediately began to flood the church.

First, a young man, who was a member of the church, walked into the Pastor's office. "This is for the amphitheater and lights," he told the Pastor as he laid over $4,000 on the Pastor's desk.

The Lord had spoken to him to give all the money he'd been saving for a vehicle as an offering to the church. "When God speaks, we have to listen," he said with a smile.

Next, there was a woman in the church who had been involved in a lawsuit in which money was owed to her. Because of the legal red tape, her attorney informed her it could be months or even years before she saw any money from the settlement.

She came into the church office with the testimony that not only had they resolved the settlement, the money had already been deposited into her account. She gave the Pastor a $5,000 tithe check from the settlement.

Shortly after that, McDonald's corporate office called the church and informed them that they were sending a grant in the amount of $10,000 to the church!

The city office was next. They contacted the church to let them know they had sent another $18,000 to be included in the church's efforts to reach the community.

It seemed that the prophetic word of the Lord was having a snowball effect as someone else walked into the church and handed the Pastor an $11,000 check for more lights and to build a play area for the children.

Praise ignited the prophetic word of the Lord. In one night it sparked a harvest that would continue to flow.

Months later, I received a text message from the Pastor again. The financial increase had continued. He was writing to give me the latest powerful testimony.

Someone had just given the church a retreat center property. Over twenty-two acres with a lodge that can accommodate over one hundred people, an indoor swimming pool, and two homes built on the property!

It's amazing what God can do by His prophetic word!

PRAISE OPENS THE DOOR
TO PROVISION

Even in the Old Testament, praise ignited the spirit of the prophets. Once, when Israel was in trouble, King Jehoshaphat asked Elisha to give them a word from the Lord. His answer?

> *". . . bring me a musician." And when the*
> *musician played, the hand of the Lord*
> *came upon him.*
>
> *2 Kings 3:15 ESV*

Praise literally provoked the prophetic word of the Lord from Elisha's spirit.

If we will faithfully praise the Lord, it activates His creation into production. This principle is clearly revealed by the Psalmist:

> *Let the peoples praise You, O God; Let*
> *all the peoples praise You. THEN THE*
> *EARTH SHALL YIELD HER INCREASE;*
> *God, our own God, shall bless us. God*
> *shall bless us, And all the ends of the*
> *earth shall fear Him.*
>
> *Psalm 67:5-7 NKJV (Emphasis added)*

What a powerful revelation. Our praise literally causes the earth to yield increase and God to release His blessings. Not just any kind of blessings, the kind that are so evident that when people see them, they immediately begin to fear God.

This literally happened for King David. He went from being a nobody to one of the richest men in the world.

When his father, Jesse, found out that Samuel the Prophet was coming to anoint a new king for Israel, he called his oldest seven sons into the house to meet Samuel and left David out in the field watching the sheep.

Just by this one action he was saying that he didn't believe David was "king material."

However, by the end of his life of praise, as his son Solomon was about to become king, David gave an offering of gold and silver from his personal treasury that would be worth over $6 billion today.

In fact, David praised God so often and so faithfully that he didn't even live long enough to receive all the favor he provoked.

God had to set up a "favor trust fund" in Heaven to hold the blessings David couldn't receive during his life on the earth.

Two hundred and seventy years after David had died, Israel was in need of God's favor and assistance. The King of Assyria had surrounded Israel with 185,000 troops and began to threaten them.

Notice what God said through the prophet Isaiah:

> *I will defend this city, to save it For My own sake and for My servant David's sake.*
>
> *2 Kings 19:34 NKJV*

David's life of praise had stored up so much favor with God that Israel was still withdrawing blessings from the account almost three hundred years later. We'll look at this principle in depth in the next chapter.

When we praise God, we are storing up favor for future generations of our own families.

Because we delight in the commandments of the Lord and fear Him, our generations will be blessed. Wealth and riches will be in their houses. (See Psalm 112:1-3.)

WORSHIP + WORD = WEALTH

In 2 Chronicles 20, we find a story of three separate armies that gathered to destroy Judah. It was a force so vast that Judah didn't have the natural resources to deal with them.

The men, women, and children of Judah gathered before the Lord. He gave them instructions to go out toward the army the next morning.

They all bowed down and began to worship the Lord. When they finished, they stood and praised God with a loud shout.

The next morning, the king appointed singers to go ahead of the army and praise the Lord.

> *At the very moment they began to sing and give praise, the Lord caused the armies of Ammon, Moab, and Mount Seir to start fighting among themselves.*
> **2 Chronicles 20:22 NLT**

When Judah arrived at the lookout point in the wilderness, all they saw were dead bodies lying on the ground as far as they could see. Not a single one of the enemy had escaped.

King Jehoshaphat and his men went out to gather the treasure that had previously belonged to their enemies. They found vast amounts of equipment, clothing, and other valuables — more than they could carry.

There was so much plunder that it took them three days just to collect it all!

Their worship released a word that brought them overwhelming wealth.

Praise and worship are dynamic elements that provoke the prophetic Word of God. Once it is released, it always brings prosperity.

As you vehemently praise God even in your private life, watch as faith rises in your spirit and you are led to speak prophetically over your house, business, and family.

You'll find yourself yielded to the Holy Spirit and He

will speak through you. You can be sure they will be words that will bring you increase and promotion.

GOD WILL NOT ALLOW PRAISING
PEOPLE TO PERISH PREMATURELY

#UnhangYourHarp

FIVE

Praise Provides Divine Protection

King David had a secret. There was an element of his life that made God describe him as "a man after my own heart" (Acts 13:22).

That blows the minds of some Christians. How could God refer to David—a man who committed both murder and adultery—as a man after His own heart?

Two things made this possible. First, David was a man who valued the presence of God and was quick to repent when he made a mistake. God can always use someone who is humble enough to repent and turn from wickedness.

Secondly, David lived a life that was dedicated to praising God. Because we are created to praise God, this meant that David was always true to his created purpose. He began in the wilderness when no one was watching him. This proves that David wasn't praising God to be seen by other people.

Because David was willing to praise God as a shepherd in the field when nobody was watching, he was able to do the same as king when an entire nation was watching him bring the Ark of the Covenant back to Jerusalem.

David began to understand how much God enjoyed hearing him worship. He must have also understood that not many people were dedicated to praising God at the same level he was.

That's when he realized he could use what God liked as leverage to initiate God's help . . . and God didn't mind at all.

Throughout the Psalms, you'll find passages where David was in trouble. David requests protection from God while praising God for His greatness.

When I first found the verse that I'm getting ready to show you, I had to stop my devotions and laugh. David was slick. He understood what made God tick and used it for his own benefit.

When David's enemies were attacking him, he cried out for God's help. But look *how* he did it:

What will you gain if I die, if I sink into the grave? Can my dust praise you? Can it tell of your faithfulness? Hear me, Lord, and have mercy on me. Help me . . .
Psalm 30:9 NLT

David was saying "I know you love my praise, but if I die, the thing you love will be gone. It's in your best interest to keep me alive so I can keep giving you praise."

Notice God didn't argue with David; He just fought on his behalf. David didn't die on a battlefield somewhere; David died of natural causes at the age of 70.

A man who fought in battle his whole life and had many enemies was not able to be killed because his praise kept him safe.

LEVERAGING THE HEART OF GOD

Almost 250 years after King David ruled over Israel, a man named Hezekiah became king over Judah. Unlike his son, Manasseh, who became king after his death, he was considered to be a righteous king who did what was pleasing to the Lord.

While his son, Manasseh, decided to reinstitute polytheistic worship (the worship of many false gods), Hezekiah gave praise and worship only to Jehovah.

His lifestyle of praise and obedience made him one of the most prominent kings in Judah's history. His name is even mentioned in the genealogy of Jesus in Matthew's Gospel.

In the fourteenth year of Hezekiah's reign, Sennacherib, who was king of Assyria (northern Iraq, northeastern Syria, southeastern Turkey, and the northwestern edges of Iran), began to attack Judah. He positioned a large force of almost 200,000 troops around Judah.

Once he had displayed his dominance and authority, he began to taunt and threaten Hezekiah and Judah. 2 Kings 19:10-12 shows us the letter he sent to Hezekiah:

> This message is for King Hezekiah of Judah. Don't let your God, in whom you trust, deceive you with promises that Jerusalem will not be captured by the king of Assyria. You know perfectly well what the kings of Assyria have done wherever they have gone. They have completely destroyed everyone who stood in their way! Why should you be any different? Have the gods of other nations rescued them—such nations as Gozan, Haran, Rezeph, and the people of Eden who were in Tel-assar? My predecessors destroyed them all!

Not only does Sennacherib threaten King Hezekiah and Judah, he also uses his letter to mock Jehovah — the Most High God.

I want you to understand that anything that threatens your safety or stands against you is also threatening the God you serve. Because you are connected to God by covenant, whatever stands against you is also standing against Him. That's why the Apostle Paul wrote to the church in Rome and said:

> *If God is for us, who can be against us?*
> **Romans 8:31 ESV**

What happened next was so vital to the protection of God's people. What Hezekiah did is a model that we can replicate in our own lives that will give us access to the supernatural protection of God.

He took the letter, went into the temple, and laid it on the altar. If this were taking place today, Hezekiah wouldn't have responded to the email, he would have just forwarded it to God's inbox.

By doing this, Hezekiah was essentially saying, "God, some of your mail was accidentally delivered to my house, so I brought it over."

He didn't want to focus on what Sennacherib said about him. Instead, he wanted to focus on what he said about God.

After he laid the letter on the altar, he began to pray a prayer of praise to God. He begins by magnifying God's position above all else:

> *God of Israel, you are enthroned between the mighty cherubim! You alone are God of all the kingdoms of the earth.*
> *2 Kings 19:15 NLT*

Hezekiah becomes an instigator. Remember that kid in school who was always trying to start fights? He would say things like, "Did you hear what he said about you? I can't believe he was talking like that about you!" Instigators do it for the sole purpose of making you mad and starting a fight. Hezekiah was doing the same to provoke a fight between Sennacherib and God:

> *Bend down, O Lord, and listen! Open your eyes, O Lord, and see! Listen to Sennacherib's words of defiance against the living God.*
> *2 Kings 19:16 NLT*

Finally, Hezekiah highlights God's greatness by comparing Him to the puny, false gods of the other pagan nations that the kings of Assyria had defeated.

Magnifying the Lord's power is one of the best ways to praise Him. We're instructed to praise Him for His mighty acts of greatness (Psalm 150:2).

Look how Hezekiah's praise described God:

> *It is true, Lord, that the kings of Assyria have destroyed all these nations. And they have thrown the gods of these nations into the fire and burned them. But of course the Assyrians could destroy them! They were not gods at all—only idols of wood and stone shaped by human hands. Now, O Lord our God, rescue us from his power; then all the kingdoms of the earth will know that you alone, O Lord, are God.*
>
> *2 Kings 19:17-19 NLT*

Hezekiah mocks the false gods of the pagans by contrasting their inability to protect their people with God's overwhelming ability to fight for His children.

When he finishes praising God, the Prophet Isaiah is stirred to speak on God's behalf and predicts Judah's deliverance from Assyria.

I love what God says to Sennacherib in response to

his mocking letter. He basically says, "Who do you think you're talking to? To Whom are you raising your voice? In case you don't know, I'll tell you. You're speaking to the Holy One of Israel!" (See 2 Kings 19:22.)

God held Sennacherib and the Assyrians in such contempt that He didn't even leave His throne to fight them Himself. In the night, He commanded one angel to descend from Heaven into the camp of the Assyrians. The angel entered the camp and killed 185,000 of the enemy soldiers.

Sennacherib packed up his camp and ran back home where he was killed by his sons in the temple of Nisroch, his false god.

God not only delivered Judah, the prophecy was fulfilled that the Assyrian army wouldn't enter Jerusalem and not even one arrow would be shot at the city.

Hezekiah's praise accessed the divine protection of God and delivered Judah from their enemies.

Please understand that when you praise God, you are provoking His intervention in your life. As God did for so many others, He will fight your battles for you.

I want to show you another secret about praise. Praise is a transaction with God that creates a supernatural account for you in Heaven.

STORED UP FAVOR

David praised God so faithfully for so long, that he didn't live long enough to reap all the benefits from his worship. As a result, God began to store David's favor in a heavenly account.

Did you know that God has what is called a *Book of Remembrance* (Malachi 3:16). When God logs your faithfulness in His book, He stores favor in your account and it's withdrawn in times of need. Look what He will do for those whose names are found in His book:

> *They shall be mine, says the Lord of hosts, in the day when I make up my treasured possession, and I will spare them as a man spares his son who serves him. Then once more you shall see the distinction between the righteous and the wicked, between one who serves God and one who does not serve him.*
> *Malachi 3:17-18 ESV*

Our faithfulness is logged within God's book and He responds to our actions accordingly. Because David didn't live long enough to retrieve all of the blessings that had been deposited into his account, those who came after him were entitled to receive them on his be-half. This was the case for Hezekiah and Judah in the story I just described to you.

The account of Sennacherib's attempted invasion of Judah took place over 270 years after David had died. As God declares He will help Hezekiah and deliver Judah from the Assyrians, notice *why* God agreed to do it:

> *I will defend this city to save it, for my*
> *own sake and for the sake of my servant*
> *David.*
>
> > *2 Kings 19:34 ESV*

How amazing! David had praised God so faithfully and had so much favor stored in his account, that God was still making withdrawals on behalf of Judah almost 300 years later. Notice that the opposite is also true:

> *. . . since you have forgotten the law of*
> *your God, I also will forget your children.*
> > *Hosea 4:6 ESV*

I've made up my mind that I'm going to honor the Word of God and His covenant to the degree that not only will I benefit from my dedication, my children and grandchildren will reap the benefits of my actions.

WHY PRAISE BRINGS PROTECTION

God's eyes function like a supernatural radar in Heaven. He is constantly searching for opportunities to help, support, and protect His people.

> *For the eyes of the Lord run to and fro*
> *throughout the whole earth, to show*
> *Himself strong on behalf of those whose*
> *heart is loyal to Him . . .*
> *2 Chronicles 16:9 NKJV*

As I wrote earlier in this book, praise is a function of love. One of the ways God can see that your heart is loyal to Him is by your praise and worship.

As you obey His command to praise Him, it shows that you're living by faith and obedience to His Word. Your obedience to God's commands gives you direct access to the manifestations of Christ's power in your everyday life (John 14:21).

Notice that Christ's supernatural power is not revealed to everyone. It's revealed to those who are faithful to the instructions of Scripture.

Praise in the face of danger brings God even more glory. This was true in the case of Shadrach, Meshach, and Abednego. In Daniel chapter 3, they faced a gruesome death because they made a choice to reserve their praise and worship for God alone. When King Nebuchadnezzar commanded everyone to bow and worship his statue, these three men refused to bend their knees.

He was so enraged that he heated his furnace seven times hotter than normal and gave them one more chance to reconsider. Their answer in the face of the impending execution was just more effusive praise to the most high God:

> *. . . our God whom we serve is able to deliver us from the burning fiery furnace, and he will deliver us out of your hand, O king.*
>
> *Daniel 3:17 ESV*

The guards bound them and threw them into the fire. However, because the fire was so hot, it killed the guards who threw them inside.

The King hurriedly jumped out of his seat and peered into the fire in amazement.

"I thought we threw three men into the fire," he said.

"We did," his counsellors replied.

"But I see *four* men walking in the midst of the fire, and they're not hurt; and the fourth looks like the son of God!" He exclaimed.

Literally, God came and inhabited their praises in the midst of the fire. God found them because His eyes had been searching for those whose hearts were loyal to Him.

When God finds you praising Him, not only does He show up to inhabit your praise (Psalm 22:3), but He comes to show His power in your life and situation.

At that point, you are dwelling in the shelter of the Most High as is described in Psalm 91. Once you are, God said regarding you:

> *I will be with him in trouble; I will rescue him and honor him. With long life I will satisfy him and show him my salvation.*
>
> *Psalms 91:15-16 ESV*

GOD IS THE ONLY ONE WHO CAN
BRING PROMOTION. AS A RESULT,
HIS FAVOR IS THE ONLY
APPROVAL WE NEED.

#UnhangYourHarp

SIX

Praise Obtains Divine Promotion

God expects you to increase. He's the only One who has the ability to promote you. He's extremely interested in promoting you.

I wanted to begin by placing those three thoughts in your mind because the impact this entire chapter will make upon your life hinges on whether or not you believe and understand them.

To bring further clarity, I want to break each thought down and show you what the Word of God says regarding these principles.

I once posted something on social media regarding supernatural promotion. I was making the point that if you will dedicate yourself to the covenant of God and obey His instructions, He will lift you head and shoulders above the rest. Almost immediately, I received an extremely religious (read offended) response from someone.

"I hope you don't mean head and shoulders above my brothers and sisters in Christ, because that would be very wrong to say," she wrote piously.

I think she was confused. Every believer is not at the same level spiritually. Our personal actions in dedication to kingdom principles will always determine how high we will rise.

Believers are at different levels spiritually because everyone is living at different levels of knowledge, faith, obedience and love. These are also the four elements that form the launching pad for our praise — and ultimately our divine promotion.

Jesus' twelve disciples weren't even all operating at the same level of faith or power. In fact, when Jesus was on a mission to raise a dead girl back to life, He only allowed three of His disciples to accompany Him to her house. (See Mark 5:35-37.)

You should never feel guilty when God promotes you even though others aren't experiencing the same increase. Divine promotion is never random. God didn't pick you because He's sovereignly favoring you above others. He is responding to your actions of obedience.

Would you feel bad when you received your paycheck after working every day for a week plus twenty extra hours of overtime while someone else who was absent from work didn't get a paycheck?

Of course not. You are being paid for your faithfulness to the company. In the same way, God rewards those who are faithful to the kingdom. Look:

> **But seek first His kingdom and His righteousness, and all these things will be added to you.**
> **Matthew 6:33 NASB**

When you put God first, He puts you first. Now let's look at the first of the three principles I gave you.

GOD EXPECTS YOU TO INCREASE

If you've studied the Word for any period of time, you'll understand that God's Kingdom is based on the principle of increase.

In Mark chapter 4, Jesus is describing how the kingdom of God functions. He explains that it's like a farmer scattering seed on the ground. Although the farmer doesn't understand how it happens, the seed turns into a blade that breaks through the ground. Then, heads of wheat are formed on the blade. Finally, the grain ripens and the harvest is reaped. That's a picture of the kingdom according to Christ — constant increase.

If we're to please God, our lives must correspond with this parable as well. The writer of Proverbs gave us a clear portrait of this principle in action:

> *But the path of the just (righteous) is like the light of dawn, That shines brighter and brighter until [it reaches its full strength and glory in] the perfect day.*
>
> *Proverbs 4:18 AMP*

Can you see the power of this passage? Our paths will steadily grow brighter until Christ returns. That means no more "down years." The roller coaster of life is over.

In the parable of the talents found in Matthew chapter 25, the master gives talents to three of his servants. To the first he gave five, to the second he gave two, and finally, to the third he gave one talent. Afterward, he left the country on business.

The first two servants invested their talents and doubled the value. However, the last servant buried his talent in the ground.

When the master returned from his trip, he was impressed with the work the first two servants had done.

But when he addressed the last servant *who refused to increase*, he wasn't just disappointed, he referred to the him as *wicked* and commanded him to be thrown into outer darkness.

Because it's God's desire that we steadily increase, anything that would hinder our increase or discourage us from pursuing it is demonic.

GOD IS THE ONLY ONE WHO CAN PROMOTE YOU

Now that we understand it's God's plan for every believer to steadily increase, we logically must search for the avenue to produce increase and find promotion.

Imagine how complex life would become if we had to leverage every personality we ever encountered in order to gain promotion and increase.

Thankfully, this is not the case. God is the only one who can bring promotion. As a result, His favor is the only approval we need.

This is extremely good news because unlike men and women whom we barely know, the Word of God sheds an enormous amount of light on God's nature, personality, likes, and dislikes.

This gives us an inside track on how to please Him.

> *For promotion cometh neither from the east, nor from the west, nor from the south. But God is the judge: he putteth down one, and setteth up another.*
>
> *Psalm 75:6-7 KJV*

It makes life so much easier knowing you only have to live to please one person. If God is pleased with your actions, it doesn't matter who is angry about them. No one can successfully oppose those whom God approves.

That's why Paul encouraged the Roman church by asking them rhetorically, "If God is for us, who can be against us?" (See Romans 8:31.)

This fact is supported strongly by what John wrote about Jesus in the Book of Revelation. He describes Jesus as the one who has the Key of David.

The Key of David has the power to open doors that no other man can shut, and it also closes (and locks) doors that no man can open. (See Revelation 3:7.)

So when Christ sees your obedience and dedication, He promised to manifest Himself to you. He will begin to open doors for you. This includes doors that others have decided should never be opened to you.

A woman who attended one of the services recently gave us a powerful promotion testimony.

Apparently, the manager of the department in which

she worked didn't like her because of the fact she was a Holy Ghost-filled Christian. When promotions became available, her manager would choose to promote her various coworkers even though she had more experience and seniority.

She became increasingly frustrated until she began to remind God that He was the one who promotes and gives favor.

Not long afterward, the corporate office made a decision to transfer her manager to a different location. In that time, she was promoted to the position of manager. Shortly thereafter, she was promoted once again.

"If that wasn't enough," she testified, "the corporate office decided to move my old manager back to our location. Now, the woman who refused to promote me is working *for* me."

God has a way of bringing you promotion when it doesn't look like promotion is available to you.

GOD IS INTERESTED IN PROMOTING YOU

God not only holds the power to bring supernatural promotion, He is extremely interested in His children going to the next level.

The writer of Hebrews describes how God interacts

with His children in order to bring them increase. Faith, the substance that comes from hearing God's Word preached, is a necessary element to fuel this interaction with God.

> *And without faith it is impossible to please him, for whoever would draw near to God must believe that he exists and that he rewards those who seek him.*
> *Hebrews 11:6 ESV*

Now we can see God's nature clearly. He has designed a reward-based system with which to interact with His children.

He has a strong desire to reward us by bringing us into constant increase and promotion.

Historically, throughout Scripture, praise is the fastest way to gain the attention of God. It is the most effective way of engaging His assistance.

PRAISE ATTRACTED THE PROPHET

When God was ready to give Israel a new king, He sent the prophet Samuel to Jesse's house to anoint one of his sons. When Samuel arrived, he inspected Jesse's seven oldest sons. Although it wasn't clear to him at first, Samuel finally realized none of the seven were to be king. I want to make this very clear: Jesse and his seven oldest sons had *nothing to do* with why the Prophet Samuel was at their house.

The reason the prophet traveled all the way to Bethlehem was because of one young man — David. When God spoke to Samuel, the choice had already been made:

> *Now the Lord said to Samuel, ". . . Fill your horn with oil and go; I will send you to Jesse the Bethlehemite, for I have selected a king for Myself among his sons."*
> *1 Samuel 16:1 NASB*

It was no accident that David was chosen to be God's ruler over the nation. When Saul failed to obey God's instructions, God searched and found someone whose heart was synchronized with His own. Samuel told Saul:

> *But now your kingdom must end, for the Lord has sought out a man after his own heart. The Lord has already appointed him to be the leader of his people, because you have not kept the Lord's command."*
> *1 Samuel 13:14 NLT*

It was David's praise that synchronized his heart to God's. His habit was to begin seeking God's presence early in the morning (Psalm 63:1).

The more time David spent in God's presence, the more God knew He could trust David with bigger tasks.

David began by taking care of the sheep. He was first promoted when he killed a lion and a bear by the power of the Spirit. After being anointed by Samuel, he was quickly promoted again into the court of King Saul where his praise won another victory over the evil spirit that troubled Saul's mind.

Soon afterward, God knew He could trust David with the task of killing Goliath and winning a national victory. It was from that moment forward that things began to accelerate in David's life.

After becoming the king, his first royal act was retrieving the Ark of the Covenant and bringing it back to Jerusalem. As they entered the city, David began to dance before God with all of his strength and led a national celebration as the anointing returned to Israel.

By the end of David's life, it was revealed that his son, Solomon, would build God's temple.

As I wrote previously, praise unlocks financial prosperity. This was the result of David's life of dedication to God. When it was time to build the temple, David made a massive withdrawal from his personal account and gave it to God. He gave 112 tons of gold and 262 tons of silver. (See 1 Chronicles 29:4.) His total offering is valued at over $6 billion today!

David went from being a shepherd whose father didn't even believe in him, to one of the greatest kings who ever lived. The vehicle that transported him through that lifelong journey was praise and worship.

Without question, praise can accomplish the same things in your life. Healing, the manifestation of God's Word, prosperity, protection, and promotion can be accessed supernaturally by a life of constant praise.

Because God is unchanging, His personality and nature remain the same. The secrets that David learned about the heart of God are still functional keys that can be used to unlock every blessing God set aside for you.

In the next section, I want to show you five habits that will ensure your praise and worship are dynamic and produce results.

Not only will you be fulfilling the command to worship in spirit and in truth, you will experience steady increase as you access the heart of the Most High God.

5 Habits of a

Dynamic Worshiper

YOU CAN ONLY BECOME DYNAMIC
BY FIRST BECOMING DISSATISFIED
WITH YOUR CURRENT LEVEL OF
DEVELOPMENT

#UnhangYourHarp

Develop Your Gift

Have you ever been in a church service when someone was about to sing a special? The nervous soloist slowly walks onto the platform and after taking the microphone gives their introduction.

I always laugh as they preface their song with the standard excuses to make sure no one expects too much from their performance.

"Would you all just pray for me today? Pastor asked me to sing this song and I haven't had much of a chance to practice this week. I woke up this morning and the devil was attacking my vocal chords, but we're going to do this song anyway, praise God. I want to encourage you, don't listen to my voice, but listen to the words of this song."

Then, the soloist proceeds to sing an off-key version of whatever song they've chosen that Sunday, and we all have to suffer through it with them.

I was actually in a service when a soloist forgot all the words to her song when she was supposed to come in. She just laid herself out "in the Spirit" on the platform until the song was over and then returned to her seat with her head down.

My question has always been, "Why didn't you practice this week?" Why is it acceptable to give God a subpar effort? What was so important in your 168-hour week that you couldn't spend one of them learning the lyrics and melody to your song?

Can you imagine a brain surgeon making those kinds of remarks before an operation?

"Now just pray for me, I haven't had time to practice this. Don't look at the actual job I do, focus on the intentions of my heart as I operate."

Laughing yet? It's ridiculous isn't it? Development of your gift is a necessity and will ensure that you never stop increasing in what God has called you to do.

DEVELOPMENT BRINGS PROMOTION

David was possibly the greatest man of praise in the

Bible. He wrote a majority of the psalms and his praise always had powerful results. He was a man after God's own heart which caused promotion throughout his entire life. He transitioned from a young, song-writing shepherd whose father didn't even believe in him, to the King of God's people in a very short time.

His dedication was the factor that allowed him to operate in such supernatural power. The psalms he wrote, the Spirit-led direction of his life, the supernatural protection he experienced, and the riches he accumulated, were all a result of his private dedication to God. He referenced his consistency in a psalm:

The degree to which you dedicate yourself to development of your gift is the degree to which doors will open in your life.

> *O God, You are my God; Early will I seek You; My soul thirsts for You; My flesh longs for You . . .*
>
> **Psalm 63:1 NKJV**

More than anything, David wanted to be in the presence of God. He made it his first pursuit every morning. It was that kind of relationship with God that caused David's praise to carry such a dynamic anointing.

Dedication to development is so important because the level at which you develop your gift is the level at which doors will open in your life and ministry.

This is how David ended up in the court of King Saul while he was still a shepherd.

> *A man's gift makes room for him, And brings him before great men.*
>
> *Proverbs 18:16 NKJV*

When King Saul's mind was being troubled by an evil spirit, he asked his servants to bring him someone who could play *skillfully* on the harp. Saul's servants immediately knew who to call.

> *One of the servants said to Saul, "One of Jesse's sons from Bethlehem is a talented harp player. Not only that . . . the Lord is with him."*
>
> *1 Samuel 16:18 NLT*

This is a perfect picture of Proverbs 18:16 in action. David's relationship with the Lord through prayer brought such an anointing on his gift that not only did he become skillful, he developed a reputation throughout the kingdom. He was the one who came to mind when someone said *"skillful harpist."*

I also want you to see that David not only had advanced skill in playing his instrument, he also carried dynamic power in his worship.

It's one thing to be a talented musician, it's an entirely different thing to be an anointed musician. Any pop artist with songs that are on the top charts travels with a skilled band. Each musician is at the top of his respective instrumental game.

While that might be the case, I don't want them as a part of my church's praise and worship team unless they're also saved and filled with the Holy Spirit.

Note: What I'm about to write next is not an excuse to be a lazy musician or singer, stop practicing and working hard, or become unfaithful to your gift. You've been warned.

Skill is not the most important element of an anointed worship service. It is important! But it's not the *most* important.

The anointing of God's Spirit is the most important element any worshiper can access. I've been a part of worship services where the one leading wasn't the most talented singer or musician, but the anointing was so strong as they worshiped.

I've also been in services where everyone on the platform was a professional and there was no anointing on the worship. It was like being at a show or a concert.

Ultimately, it's God's Spirit that makes the difference in any atmosphere. His Spirit is the only thing that can bring freedom to any man or woman. His presence alone carries power. (See 2 Corinthians 3:17.)

We are, however, commanded to strive for skill. After all, God deserves our best. The Psalmist wrote:

> *Sing to Him a new song; Play skillfully with a shout of joy.*
>
> *Psalm 33:3 NKJV*

This falls under the heading of stewardship. If God gives you a gift, He expects you to increase it.

HOW I RECEIVED MY GIFT FROM GOD

When I was in my young teens, my father spent time traveling and ministering with Evangelist R.W. Schambach who was a mighty revivalist.

In his tent meetings there was always powerful, Pentecostal praise and worship—which I loved. Upbeat, happy, deliverance music that you could dance to. Drums, bass, keyboard, and my favorite, the Gospel B3 Hammond organ and Leslie speaker.

(It's been argued by many Pentecostals that you can't even have a proper service without a B3 Hammond organ in the room.)

I would stand on the front row and dance every night through the entire praise and worship service. When I got a little more boldness, I crept around the back of the platform and would stand next to the edge and watch the organist play.

I'm not quite sure how, but I eventually found a seat on the bench next to the organist each night. I would watch in amazement at how "Wild" Willie Isaac (the organist) and Lance Palmer (the keyboardist and worship leader) would play their instruments.

I loved it and I wanted to be able to play like they did. Brother Schambach would come out on the platform and see me sitting over there every night and just smile.

In the final service of the ten-day crusades Brother Schambach would hold under the tent, he would have a children's blessing service.

It was in one of those services as I walked through the prayer line with thousands of others, that Brother Schambach stopped and laid his hands on me.

He prayed that from that night forward the Anointing would come upon my life to play and sing the same kind of Pentecostal music that I loved so much.

Looking back, I realize now that after he laid hands on me, the Spirit of the Lord came mightily upon me from that day forward. (See 1 Samuel 16:13.)

THE PROCESS OF DEVELOPMENT

Not long after that, someone gave me the first keyboard I ever owned—a Roland D-50 synthesizer that I still have to this day.

I want you to understand that after Brother Schambach laid hands on me, I didn't immediately go to the keyboard and begin to play it supernaturally or unaware of what chords I was playing.

Instead, God anointed my mind to retain knowledge. This verse of Scripture came to my spirit:

> *Work hard so you can present yourself to God and receive his approval. Be a good worker, one who does not need to be ashamed and who correctly explains the word of truth.*
>
> *2 Timothy 2:15 NLT*

Although this Scripture is in reference to studying and handling the Word of God, the principle remains true. You've got to be a good steward of the talent God places in your hands.

Don't take the talent He has blessed you with and bury it in the ground like the foolish servant did in Jesus' parable of the talents. (See Matthew 25:14-30.)

In that parable, when the master returned home and questioned the foolish servant and found out that he buried his talent and had no increase to show for it, he regarded him as *wicked*.

It's truly wrong to receive a gift from God but not give it any of your effort or attention. As believers, we are designed to steadily increase in every area of our lives until Jesus returns. (See Proverbs 4:18.)

After I got my Roland D-50, I set it up in my room, grabbed some headphones, and began playing it for hours at a time.

I would come home from school and sit in my room playing that old keyboard while learning new songs and chord progressions.

God anointed my mind so that whenever I learned something new, I never forgot it.

There was no YouTube when I started playing in 1997, so when I heard other keyboard players playing chords or progressions that I liked, I would ask them to show me how to play them.

Then, I would go home and learn those chords or

progressions in every key. I also went to a bookstore and bought a chord dictionary so that I could learn how to play every chord there was and learn their names.

I was excited to develop the gift God had given me. To this day, I have not lost my excitement for my gift.

I still sit at a piano in my house and play and worship God for hours at a time. Although I've been leading worship for about twenty years at the time of this writing, I'm still actively seeking to develop my gift.

If you ask my wife, she'll tell you that many nights she'll wake up and see me in the glow of my phone or iPad watching tutorial videos and learning new things that I can use to go to the next level.

I want to give you four practical steps to develop your gift successfully.

1. DISSATISFACTION

My grandfather, who pastored for over sixty years, had a quote that I'll never forget. He said, "I'm satisfied with a dissatisfied satisfaction."

The point he was making was that although he was happy with where God had brought him up to that point, he knew it wasn't the end of his increase.

It's dangerous to become satisfied with where you

are in life. There's always a greater level waiting for you.

As author Jim Collins asserts in his best-selling book *Good to Great,* the reason so many corporations never become great companies is because they're satisfied with being good companies.

The same is true for any gifted believer. If you stay happy with where you are, you'll never pursue a greater level. You must become dissatisfied with your current level of development. That's how Paul thought.

> *I don't mean to say that I have already achieved these things or that I have already reached perfection. But I press on to possess that perfection for which Christ Jesus first possessed me.*
>
> *Philippians 3:12 NLT*

Paul went on to say that he disciplined himself to forget the past and look forward to what lies ahead (Philippians 3:13).

Take a moment and thank God for how far you've come in your development already — now forget it.

It's time to press toward a new level in your gift. One of the best ways to stay dissatisfied is to surround yourself with people who are far ahead of you in the same area of gifting or calling. They give you direction.

2. DIRECTION

Paul used himself as a role model for the new believers in the churches he planted. He instructed them to watch him and then copy his actions as he followed Jesus (1 Corinthians 11:1). The reason for this is he was far more advanced in his Christianity than they were. He was much more mature in his gifts and calling, and he was far more fruitful.

Having someone who you can watch produce at a higher level than you're producing makes it so much easier to level up. They're not only doing what you *want* to do, they can also show you *how* to get there.

It's now easier than ever to learn from the best. The internet has become the fundamental tool of learning. From tutorial sites like *lynda.com* and *masterclass.com*, to my personal favorite, YouTube, you can learn anything you desire online.

For musicians and singers, there's an endless amount of free content online that will take you higher if you're willing to spend the time searching for it.

The point I'm making is that the person who gives you direction to the next level doesn't have to be sitting in front of you. You don't necessarily need to pay for vocal or instrument lessons.

I personally have never taken a formal piano lesson

in my entire life. I've spent my time searching out the information I need to develop.

You can do the same. The key is staying diligent in your search for the next level.

3. DILIGENCE

I'm surprised when gifted people are unaware of the top names in their area of gifting. They're oblivious.

If you're a bass player, you should know names like John Patitucci, Victor Wooten, Jaco Pastorius, Stanley Clarke, and Marcus Miller.

For example, if I was a bass player, I would begin by taking the five names above and finding every YouTube clip of their performances that I could.

Then, I would slowly break down each video and learn to do exactly what they did in that performance (there are people on YouTube who create many of these tutorials for you).

You could easily spend five years just completing that project. Imagine if you could duplicate the bass styles of five of the greatest bass players who ever lived.

What would happen is that not only would your skill level dramatically increase, but you would begin to think about playing in the way that they thought about it. Your personal style would be developed around the greatest styles of all time.

In the process of learning their licks and grooves, your timing, accuracy, dexterity, and rhythm would become honed like a sharp blade.

Diligence is the nonstop pursuit of greatness.

4. DISCIPLINE

Once you've completed the previous three steps, you'll find yourself in the place where most people stop. It's easy to know there's a greater level available and to watch greater people in action. Most people even know what they must do to obtain their goals.

For example, everyone knows what it takes to lose weight: consume less calories than your body burns. The art of losing weight is not a mystery, yet 70% of Americans are obese or overweight.

This is because knowing what to do and actually doing it are two very different things.

If you're going to go to another level, you've got to do what other people aren't willing to do. You have to discipline yourself and make development a priority in your life.

As financial advisor Dave Ramsey often says, "Live

like no one else now so that later you can live like no one
else." The point he's making is that if you'll discipline
yourself in a way that no one else is willing to do, later,
you'll be living at a level that very few people have at-
tained in life.

The Apostle Paul was very aware of this concept. He
knew that if he did what he wanted to do instead of
what he should do, he would lose his rewards.

> *I discipline my body like an athlete,
> training it to do what it should. Other-
> wise, I fear that after preaching to others
> I myself might be disqualified.*
> **1 Corinthians 9:27 NLT**

Paul knew he wouldn't *feel* like pursuing his calling. People get tired, bored, and frustrated. Discipline
is what keeps you pushing toward the next level even in
times where you don't feel the excitement you once did.

The secret of your success is hidden in the habits of
your daily routine.

Time provides an even playing field for everyone. We
all have twenty-four hours in our day. The question is
what will we do with the time we've been given?

Time is the most valuable resource you have. It's a
resource you can never get back. What will you do with

your time that will ensure you level up?

Don't sleep your time away. Don't fill your time with the distraction of entertainment. Don't waste your most valuable resource.

> *Do you see a man skillful in his work?*
> *He will stand before kings; he will not*
> *stand before obscure men.*
> *Proverbs 22:29 ESV*

Notice, people who become skillful by discipline and dedication will never stand in obscurity. Greatness brings you to the forefront in any arena.

Once again, your gift will make room for you and bring you before great men (Proverbs 18:16).

A FINAL WORD ON DEVELOPMENT

One of the reasons I believe God has continued to increase my gift rapidly as I pursue it in dedication is because of a vow I made to Him.

I promised Him that if He would gift me and anoint me, I would never use my gift for anyone but Him.

I don't play coffee houses, do secular concerts, or put together weekend bar bands for extra money. I'd never go on tour with a secular artist no matter how good the paycheck was.

You may think that's crazy, but I know worship leaders who have done all of those things. My gift isn't for any of that. My gift is for God alone.

If you'll also make that vow to God and keep it, I believe He'll give you exponential increase and continue to promote you throughout your entire life.

Promotion only comes from the Lord (Psalm 75:6-7).

FASTING AND PRAYER ALLOW
YOU TO ACTIVATE THE FULL
IMPARTATION OF POWER YOU'VE
RECEIVED FROM GOD

#UnhangYourHarp

HABIT TWO

Engage in Prayer & Fasting

It has happened so many times that it's like a broken record in my mind. I'm standing on the front row of a church service about to take the microphone and preach, and the worship leader launches into a prayer as he transitions between songs . . .

"Father God, we just come to you now, Father God. We thank you, Father God, for your goodness, Father God. And we know, Father God, that you're here, Father God. We ask you, Father God, to just fill us up, Father God, until we overflow, Father God."

The only difference with the example I just gave is that, sadly, it's much more coherent than the prayers I've heard in the past.

When someone prays publicly, it becomes very evident whether or not they pray privately. Many times, the lack of a personal prayer life leaves your public prayers forced and awkward.

You're finally addressing someone you should have spoken with throughout the week, but you haven't talked to for a long time. As a result, you have to use filler words to give yourself extra time to figure out what you're going to say next.

What would someone think if you held a normal conversation with them like that?

"Hi Jim, I just wanted to ask you, oh Jim, if you'd like to go to lunch, oh Jim. We could get some Mexican, oh Jim. I'd like to just catch up, oh Jim. And I'd like to ask you right now, oh Jim, if you'd like to take one car to the restaurant, oh Jim . . ."

They would look at you like you'd lost your mind.

In fact, if you'll notice, you can tell when two people talk often. There's a familiarity as they speak. They laugh at the same things and have their own inside jokes.

The prompting to praise God, and the power of your praise are byproducts of your personal prayer life because you develop a familiarity with God and His presence — and that makes all the difference.

Familiarity brings you to a place of comfort. Your familiarity with the presence of God removes any anxiety about interacting with Him. This is because love is the driving force behind seeking His presence.

The Word of God tells us that perfect love drives out fear (1 John 4:18). Spending time in prayer allows you to experience the landscape of God's presence personally. This is extremely important as a worship leader.

BE A TOUR GUIDE NOT A TOURIST

The term *worship leader* suggests that you are going to guide people into a place of praise and worship. That means you have to be familiar with the landscape of meaningful, engaging worship, and dynamic, breakthrough praise.

Imagine booking your first safari in the jungles of Africa. You finally land and drive out into the wilderness ready to see dangerous animals you've never encountered before.

Finally, after having traveled in the Jeep for over an hour, you ask your guide if you're getting close to the destination.

"I don't know," he replies. "This is my first time on the continent of Africa, as well."

He's completely unqualified to be your guide. He doesn't know the terrain. He's unfamiliar with the culture and you'll likely end up lost.

That's what happens in many churches today. Leaders are not equipped to guide anyone into the presence of God because they themselves haven't been there. How can you lead someone somewhere you've never been? You can't.

The best you can do in that situation is *perform*. Worship becomes a soulish concert. Everyone ends up watching the worship team and becomes completely disengaged. This is completely contrary to how we're instructed to worship God.

> *God is Spirit, and those who worship*
> *Him must worship in spirit and truth.*
> *John 4:24 NKJV*

If I look out across the crowd and people are standing with their hands on the back of the chair in front of them, sitting down, or just scrolling through Instagram, I'm failing as a worship leader.

As worship leaders, we must be anointed enough to bring the presence of God into the room with us, and then pull those who have come to church into the power of His presence.

We must access the spirit realm when we praise and worship God. Prayer and fasting are the keys that allow you to become familiar with the landscape of God's presence ahead of time.

One of the reasons God was able to use David in such a mighty way, is because David's spirit was so sensitive to God's spirit. Notice that when David arrived at the battlefield where Goliath was taunting Israel, David became grieved when He heard Goliath's blasphemy. As soon as he heard the way Goliath mocked the God of Israel, he immediately wanted to destroy him.

The reason the other soldiers didn't have the same intense desire to destroy Goliath is because they didn't have the same intense love for God that David did.

David had spent many hours alone in the field praying, singing, playing his harp, and writing psalms. He had a close, personal relationship with God.

How did David know there was fullness of joy in God's presence? How did he know you could taste and see the Lord's goodness before you got to Heaven?

The reason David could describe the wonderful benefits and attributes of God's presence is because he had been there many times.

THE INTERACTIVE EXPERIENCE

It was this kind of relationship that brought God's delivering presence into King Saul's court the moment David began playing his harp (1 Samuel 16:23).

Notice, prayer — and times of fasting — are interactive elements. They provoke God and release His power in your life. David's consistent dedication to the presence of God meant that he carried the power of God with him. Furthermore, he was aware of God's presence wherever he went.

> *Where can I go to escape Your Spirit?*
> *Where can I flee from Your presence?*
> **Psalm 139:7 HCSB**

The same was true for Christ. After forty days of fasting and prayer in the wilderness, He returned in the power of the Holy Spirit, and His ministry of signs and wonders began (Luke 4:14).

It was Christ's dedication to prayer and fasting that allowed Him to operate in the miracle-working power of God on a daily basis.

He transferred this ability to His disciples so that they could perform the same level of miracles that He did. The only problem was, they had His *power*, but they lacked His *dedication*.

On one occasion, parents brought their son to be healed by the disciples. He was possessed by a demon spirit that often tried to kill him. The disciples tried unsuccessfully to heal the boy.

When Jesus heard about this, He rebuked them and then quickly healed the boy and cast the spirit out of him. The disciples were confused. Later, they asked Jesus why they had no success in their attempts to cast that particular spirit out. Jesus answered them by comparing their dedication to His own:

> *So He said to them, "This kind can come out by nothing but prayer and fasting."*
> *Mark 9:29 NKJV*

We can clearly see that the disciples didn't have the same dedication to prayer that Jesus had. As a result, although they had a direct impartation of power from Jesus, they couldn't fully activate it.

The level of power you release as a believer is directly connected to the amount of time you dedicate to prayer.

The level of power you release as a believer is directly connected to the amount of time you dedicate to prayer.

In Matthew chapter 26, Jesus leads the disciples into a garden to pray. Once they had entered the garden, He went further and left them alone.

He returned an hour later and found them all asleep. He woke them, encouraged them to pray, and left them again. Afterward, He had to return and wake them up two more times.

Clearly, it was the disciples lack of prayer that short circuited their power. I've often said that because Jesus was completely yielded to the Father's will, if He didn't hear His Father speaking through prayer, He would have been mute.

> *. . . I do nothing on my own authority,*
> *but speak just as the Father taught me.*
> *John 8:28 ESV*

Prayer makes Christianity an interactive experience. No other religion or false god can hear prayers, answer prayers, or do anything as the result of prayers. Only our God — who is alive — has the ability to interact with us through this powerful system.

THE APOSTOLIC JAILBREAK

Prayer and praise, when coupled together, produce a dynamic result. Adding praise to your prayers is like throwing gasoline on a fire. These are two elements that were created to be used together.

In Acts chapter 16, Paul and Silas were thrown into

jail for bringing deliverance to a slave girl who was a fortune teller. Those who owned her were angry that their avenue to make money from her abilities had suddenly vanished. As a way of revenge, they began to tell lies about Paul and Silas so that they were imprisoned by the Romans.

After being severely beaten, Paul and Silas were locked in the inner dungeon of the prison. Around midnight, they were praying and singing praises unto God. Suddenly, a massive earthquake shook the jail. Every door swung open and everyone's chains fell off.

The jailer and his entire household were saved and baptized as a result of that miracle. Not only that, but the city officials came and personally apologized to Paul and Silas.

Prayer and praise turned their entire situation around in a matter of moments. Many times, the chains that need to be broken and the doors that need to be opened aren't visible, but invisible.

King Saul was being harassed by an evil spirit that was troubling his mind. He was bound with invisible chains and locked in a prison that cannot be seen by the naked eye.

However, David's dedication to prayer and praise released the anointing, broke the demonic chains, and opened the door to that invisible prison.

Every dynamic worship leader understands this ability and is willing to dedicate themselves to prayer and fasting so that others can be set free.

Did you notice that as Paul and Silas began praying and praising God and the earthquake shook the jail, their cell door was not the only one that opened? Did you see that their chains weren't the only chains to fall off?

The Bible says that *every* door came open and *every* chain fell off. This is because praise and worship can have an overflowing effect.

David spent his entire life praising God. That praise not only brought anointing, blessing, favor, and wisdom to him, these benefits also came to his son, Solomon.

While David fought and struggled for victory his entire life, Solomon did not have to:

> *But the Lord said to me, 'You have killed many men in the battles you have fought . . . But you will have a son who will be a man of peace. I will give him peace with his enemies in all the surrounding lands . . . and I will give peace and quiet to Israel during his reign.*
>
> *1 Chronicles 22:8-9 NLT*

Notice that David's life of praise allowed him to transfer spiritual blessings to his son that cannot be bought with money.

THE BENEFITS OF FASTING

In my previous book, *Blood on the Door,* I examined what God spoke through the prophet Isaiah to the people of Israel. He gave them instructions about fasting and prayer and revealed the benefits that would result from their obedience.

As we take a closer look at what God said in Isaiah chapter 58, we'll see that there are five distinct blessings that are released when we engage His presence in fasting and prayer. Let's look at the Scriptures describing the benefits of God's chosen fast:

> *Then your light shall break forth like the morning, Your healing shall spring forth speedily, And your righteousness shall go before you; The glory of the Lord shall be your rear guard. Then you shall call, and the Lord will answer.*
>
> *Isaiah 58:8,9 NKJV*

1. Your light shall break forth like the morning. When the Bible speaks of light, it is speaking of revelation knowledge. Divine understanding of God's Word sets us on another level in the supernatural realm.

David said that God's Word became a lamp for his feet and a light unto his path (Psalm 119:105). Your level of understanding of God's Word determines the level of freedom you will experience in your life (John 8:32).

Your success and power in worship is determined by your revelation and understanding of Scripture. Because God's Word is the basis upon which we receive our breakthroughs, it must fill us as we worship Him.

2. Your healing shall spring forth speedily. The second thing clearly promised as a benefit of fasting and prayer is that divine healing will quickly manifest in your body.

Not only will you receive healing virtue, but you will be empowered to release healing virtue to those who need it as you worship.

3. Your righteousness shall go before you. The prophet Jeremiah declared that the Lord is our righteousness (Jeremiah 23:6). This means that the Lord will go ahead of us and prepare the way, warn us of things to come, and fight on our behalf.

A perfect picture of this happening is when the Lord

spoke to King Cyrus through the prophet Isaiah. He assured him of success when He said:

> *I will go before you, Cyrus, and level the mountains. I will smash down gates of bronze and cut through bars of iron. And I will give you treasures hidden in the darkness — secret riches.*
>
> *Isaiah 45:2-3 NLT*

Every hindrance that stands in your way will be leveled by the power of God. One translation of this passage says that God will "make the crooked places straight." This has special significance because when your path is crooked, it slows your momentum.

As you lead others in praise and worship, every hindrance sent from the enemy to disrupt the atmosphere of praise will be destroyed by the Almighty God.

4. The glory of the Lord shall be your rear guard. He protects us from behind no matter what our enemy may have planned to destroy us.

It's a wonderful thing to know that God's got your back. He never wants to see us fail, but many times we're so busy with the details of life that we don't hear His voice, or we don't petition Him by faith to receive secrets about the future (Jeremiah 33:3).

Remember, everything we receive from God must be received by faith. If actions of faith are not present, there is nothing to motivate God to move on our behalf.

Prayer and fasting are faith actions that motivate God to reveal hidden things regarding our future. According to the book of James, one of the main reasons we don't have what God has prepared for us is because we fail to ask Him for it (James 4:3).

5. Then shall you call, and the Lord will answer. One of the wonderful benefits of prayer coupled with fasting that we see throughout the Word of God is that it expedites the answers to our prayers.

While we as New Testament believers may not need to fast to have our prayers answered, there is no question that fasting is a powerful supplement to our prayers.

It's important to understand that God doesn't reward every believer. He rewards those who diligently seek His face (Hebrews 11:6).

Fasting and prayer are undeniable access points into the presence of God and proof that you are seeking Him diligently. God spoke to the prophet Jeremiah and said:

> *And you will seek Me and find Me, when*
> *you search for Me with all your heart. I*

will be found by you, says the Lord.
Jeremiah 29:13-14 NKJV

I want to encourage you to become a spiritual worshiper. This is not a job or a hobby; it's a calling. You have to make up your mind — as David did — that you will be anointed with fresh oil (Psalm 92:10).

By dedicating yourself to daily prayer and scheduled fasting throughout your year, you are showing God that you are diligently seeking Him and your heart belongs to Him.

When He sees that, He will show Himself strong and mighty on your behalf (2 Chronicles 16:9).

BY FILLING YOURSELF WITH THE
ETERNAL POWER OF SCRIPTURE,
YOU ENSURE THAT YOU WILL
OVERFLOW WITH A
LIFE-GIVING SUBSTANCE

#UnhangYourHarp

Feed Yourself Fresh Bread

Earlier in my ministry, because people knew that I was a praise and worship leader, churches would call me before I came to hold a revival to see if there were any songs I wanted them to sing during the meeting.

I would always tell them to just do what they always did and I'm sure it would be fine. But when I would arrive and begin the meeting, a similar issue would arise and I saw a pattern in many of the churches in which I preached.

It would happen like this. I would announce that we were going to have a healing service and I would tell the congregation which night it was going to be.

When that night came, the worship team would play through the set of songs they had planned, but without fail, each church would choose the same song to sing either right before I preached, or while I was ministering to the sick.

I had no issue with the majority of the song, but when it came time to sing the bridge, the words always grated at my spirit. Quoting from the book of Job, the lyrics say that God "gives and takes away."

While this is found in the Bible (Job 1:21), it is something Job said in ignorance. His doctrine and thoughts about God were wrong. God doesn't take good things like health and blessings out of our lives; He adds them to our lives.

In fact, every good and perfect gift come to us directly from God above (James 1:17). As a result of his foolish speaking, a man named Elihu rebukes Job for six consecutive chapters. When he's finished, God speaks and begins to rebuke Job.

By the end, Job realizes his ignorance and asks God for forgiveness:

> *I was talking about things I knew nothing about, things far too wonderful for me . . . I take back everything I said, and I sit in dust and ashes to show my repentance.*
>
> *Job 42:3,6 NLT*

Meanwhile, I had to sit back and endure this unscriptural part of the song over and again before ministering healing to people.

I would get frustrated. It was almost like you could feel the faith for miracles being sucked from the room.

Why is that? Well, imagine if someone wrote a song about you and the content of the song was a description of your character. The song goes like this:

Jennifer is a thief. If there's anything good or valuable in your house, hide it. Because Jenny's coming over with her sticky little fingers and she'll rob you blind. Oh! Jennifer is a thief. Jennifer is a thief . . .

How long do you think Jennifer is going to stick around as everybody joins in on the chorus slanderously singing about her character? Not long.

In the same way, why would God stay around as the congregation sings about the fact that He gives health and blessings and then takes them away?

It's important to remember there are things we can say and do that will grieve (Ephesians 4:30) or stifle (1 Thessalonians 5:19) the Holy Spirit.

As God's Word and the Holy Spirit are the most important gifts we've ever been given after Christ, we must honor them with every part of our lives—that even includes the songs we sing.

I remember the final time I allowed this to happen in one of my services. I was standing on the front row preparing to preach when I heard the opening intro to my nemesis song.

By the time they got to the bridge, I'd had enough. Although I had another message prepared to preach, I sat down on the pew while the song continued and wrote a new message for that service.

My new message title was "He gives and takes away." I preached that day on all the things God gives (life, health, strength, peace, joy, blessing), and all of the things He takes away (sickness, poverty, anxiety, depression, etc).

We've got to honor God by properly representing His character and nature. Now when churches call me and ask if there are any songs I'd like them to sing while I'm there, I reply, "No. But there are a few I'd like you not to sing . . ."

EXPERIENCE MY OVERFLOW

One of the reasons it's so vital to be filled with the Word of God is because as a worshiper, it's important to govern what is flowing out of you. God's Word is clear that the substance which fills our hearts will flow out of us:

> *Whatever is in your heart determines what you say. A good person produces good things from the treasury of a good heart, and an evil person produces evil things from the treasury of an evil heart.*
>
> *Matthew 12:34-35 NLT*

When someone hasn't filled their heart with content from the Word of God, whatever has been happening in their life floods out of their mouth.

God has a specific way that we are to praise and worship Him. John's Gospel tells us that we must worship God in spirit and in truth (John 4:24).

True, spiritual worship is based upon God's Word. The Word of God is the only spiritual truth there is. I want you to see that it's not just truth, it's also divine life flowing from your spirit. Our praise and worship should impart supernatural life to others as well as ourselves. Look what Jesus said regarding His Word:

> *The words that I speak to you are spirit, and they are life.*
>
> *John 6:63 NKJV*

I want you to notice that when we fill our spirits with the mighty Word of God, as we begin to worship, the Word flows out of us.

Because the Word is flowing out of us, divine life is also being imparted to those around us.

Word-based worship is one of the main keys to breakthrough. I refuse to sing anything that isn't scriptural. If I hear any song that has a confession that isn't congruent with the Word of God, I refuse to sing it.

Through the years, I've heard songs declaring that we're still just sinners saved by grace, songs about how hard life is, and many other things that don't line up with God's Word.

I'm constantly wondering how Christians can sing songs with lyrics that directly contradict God's Word.

Alarm bells should go off in your spirit when you hear things like that. The Psalmist wrote that the entrance of God's Word brings light and causes understanding to come — even to the unwise (Psalm 119:130). As God's Word continues to fill you, it will immediately become clear when something is being said that is out of alignment with God's will.

It may seem like I'm just being a stickler on this subject, but whether or not we follow this principle determines whether or not we see God's supernatural power manifested through our praise and worship.

GOD IS WATCHING

God is not required to do anything other than what He said He would do. His Word is the perfect picture and representation of His will.

God doesn't randomly manifest His presence. It's not an accident when miracles take place. The power of God's presence is revealed in response to faith in His Word. In fact, God is watching to see if you're speaking His mighty Word. When He sees you speak, He begins to perform.

> *Then the Lord said to me, "You have seen well, for I am watching over My word to perform it."*
> *Jeremiah 1:12 NASB*

Notice that God is only required to perform His Word. Only when our words are synchronized with His do we see the manifestations of His power.

That's why our praise and worship should be based upon and filled with Scripture. Once you remove the element of God's Word from your life, you remove the supernatural aspect of Christianity as well.

As I mentioned previously, the Psalmist wrote that God's Word brings understanding:

> *The entrance of Your words gives light; It*
> *gives understanding to the simple.*
> **Psalm 119:130 NKJV**

Without that understanding, the light of God's presence and power is removed. When His presence is absent, your life will look the same as someone who doesn't have a relationship with God. Look at this:

> *A man who wanders from the way of understanding will rest in the assembly of the dead.*
> **Proverbs 21:16 NKJV**

That's a mind-blowing truth! What the writer of Proverbs is telling us is that you can be a follower of God, but if you don't have the understanding of His Word in your spirit, your life will look the same as someone who doesn't belong to God.

Although you have a Redeemer who saved you, healed you, provided prosperity for you, and delivered peace and joy to you, if you don't have a revelation of those things, they won't be a reality in your life.

As I wrote in *Blood on the Door*, the lives of those who have been redeemed shouldn't look the same as those who don't have a Redeemer.

It's the Word of God that gives you access to every aspect of your redemption. He is actively seeking those who love Him so that He can perform supernaturally in their lives:

> *For the eyes of Yahweh roam throughout the earth to show Himself strong for those whose hearts are completely His.*
> *2 Chronicles 16:9 HCSB*

Jesus taught that obedience is the evidence that proves someone loves Him (John 14:21).

Without the Word, we have no access to the mighty acts of God.

When you fill yourself with the eternal power of Scripture, you are ensuring that you will overflow with a life-giving substance at all times. A worshiper who makes the Word a priority in their life won't have to struggle to live in victory.

In a short period of time you can see breakthrough while others may struggle through the same issues for many years. This is why the Psalmist wrote:

> *A single day in your courts is better than a thousand anywhere else!*
> *Psalm 84:10 NLT*

In a short period of time in the presence of God can produce much more than years of striving for an answer on your own. Jesus is the Word of God (John 1:14).

Jesus taught that He is the Bread of Life (John 6:35). When you fill yourself with the Word, you're filling yourself with fresh bread.

This means you'll always have the ability to refresh others. This is a cyclical process. It's a never-ending flow of encouragement.

> *The generous will prosper; those who re-*
> *fresh others will themselves be refreshed.*
> *Proverbs 11:25 NLT*

Seek Out Supernatural Impartation

Recently, Carolyn and I took our oldest daughter, Madelyn, to Universal Studios for her birthday. As many parents know, amusement parks are fun . . . for about the first two or three hours.

After that, the heat, jam-packed restaurants, nine-dollar bottles of water, and ninety-minute waits for each ride become overbearing.

For the first time, we chose to stay at one of the Universal Studios resort hotels. Rather than fighting traffic to leave the park and wade through the concrete jungle to an off-site hotel, we only had a short boat ride from the front entrance of the park back to our room.

We quickly learned about another benefit that we had never experienced before — the Universal Express Pass.

The Express Pass gives you access to a separate entrance to each attraction in the park. Furthermore, there are no limits to how many times you can use the pass or which rides will accept it.

I didn't fully understand the power of the pass until we arrived at the entrance of one of the most popular attractions in the entire park.

Although I was there so that my kids could have fun, I wasn't looking forward to that long, arduous walk to the front of the line. I think every parent can sympathize with the dread you feel when you look at the digital clock that displays the current wait time for the ride.

Here we go again. I thought to myself as I looked at the wait time: *85 minutes.*

Then I saw a separate entrance bearing the same Express Pass logo that was printed on the credit card-style passes the hotel staff had given us that morning.

"Passes please," the attendant said as we walked toward the entrance. I quickly pulled the cards out of my pocket and she scanned them at the gate.

As we entered, I realized that there was basically no line. We moved quickly through the queue and advanced to the front of the line in no time. Like any competitive dad, I timed our wait in the express lane so that later I could brag about how fast it was.

A line that should have taken us 85 minutes to navigate only took us 7 minutes to complete.

After we finished the ride, my daughter wanted to ride it again. Now that I knew we could advance quickly, I didn't have to come up with a reason why we had to wait until later because I didn't want to stand in another 85-minute line. We simply got back in the Express Pass line.

As we rapidly advanced to the front again, I saw that we were passing people in line that we'd just passed moments before. We would finish the ride twice before most people in line had ridden it once. We were enjoying a promotion-based benefit that many others weren't.

The Express Pass works in much the same way that supernatural impartation works. It allows you to go further faster.

FURTHER FASTER

Impartation is a force that God designed to ensure each generation of His children doesn't have to begin at the ground level. The Kingdom of God is based upon increase. That means each generation should begin at a higher level of revelation and power than the previous generation did.

We understand that the same principle is true even

outside of the supernatural realm. Maybe when you were growing up, your family struggled financially. You felt the pain of being poor and made a decision that you would do whatever it took to make sure your children never had to experience poverty.

Although you may have started your adult life in debt and with nothing in savings, you worked and disciplined yourself to eliminate debt and save money to be a blessing to your children.

As they get older, they will benefit from all the valuable bits of wisdom you've gleaned from a lifetime of learning. Your children will be able to receive an inheritance that you've set aside for them.

Now, when it's time for your children to begin their adult lives, they won't have to start in debt and living from paycheck to paycheck. They can begin not only with the resources you've left them, they also have the knowledge of how you succeeded.

That is impartation. It is giving someone something that they didn't generate on their own.

How foolish would it be to make your children spend forty years (that you've already spent) learning the principles it takes to get where you are now. You could easily teach them what you know which would allow them to begin on your current level and build to a higher level from there.

As my pastor, Bishop Rick Thomas, says regarding the next generation, "My ceiling should be their floor."

That is the biblical method of advancement in God's kingdom. God doesn't want you to continually try and fail until you learn the right way to do something.

God doesn't want His children to learn by *destruction*; He wants them to learn by *instruction*.

Imagine what kind of a father I would be if I saw my young son, who is not yet two, climbing up onto the counter to stick his little hand into a hot toaster oven.

"Go ahead and touch it," I shout to him. "You won't try that again, will you?"

That's negligence and abuse. A loving father would shout a warning and run to stop his child from touching what would hurt him.

God established the system of impartation so that we could learn by observation and instruction. Through this method, we can advance with momentum in the kingdom of God. It requires a special ingredient in your heart—*hunger*.

TWO SCOOPS ARE BETTER THAN ONE

In the Old Testament, there was a prophet named Elijah. He was the powerful man of God who called fire down from Heaven in the contest with the prophets of Baal. He saw mighty miracles take place throughout his ministry. He wasn't just a prophet, he was more of a *professor prophet*.

In those days, there was a school of prophets founded by Samuel. They were also known as the "company of prophets" or the "sons of the prophets."

In fact, on his final journey before being taken into Heaven, Elijah stopped in two cities that apparently housed campuses of the prophetic school: Jericho and Bethel (2 Kings 2:1-5).

Elisha, Elijah's assistant and understudy, asked him for a double portion of his spirit. Although Elijah told him it was a difficult request, he said it would be granted if Elisha saw him when he was taken into Heaven.

At that moment, Elisha made a decision to pursue the impartation of Elijah's gift. He wanted what Elijah had. Notice that as they travel from Gilgal to Bethel and from Bethel to Jericho, these other prophets emerged to give Elisha a prophetic word about his master.

"Don't you know your master is going to be taken away from you today?" They asked him. (See 2 Kings 2:3,5.) I want you to see that although these men were truly prophets who had received teaching from Elijah and knew that he was about to leave the earth, they didn't have the hunger to petition him for the same impartation that Elisha did. They stayed where they were while Elisha would not leave Elijah's side until he received what he asked for.

The actions of the sons of the prophets is a picture of complacency and laziness. They thought they had all they needed and were satisfied to stay at the current level. Elisha, however, wanted to go higher.

He didn't just want to *replicate* Elijah's ministry; he wanted to have a double portion of production.

In the final moments of their journey, they came to the Jordan River. Using his mantle, Elijah struck the water. The river parted and he and Elisha crossed on dry ground. After they reached the other side, a chariot of fire came and took Elijah to Heaven in a whirlwind.

Before he ascended, however, he dropped his mantle — the symbol of his power — down to Elisha.

Elisha picked it up and walked back to the Jordan River. It was now time to prove the impartation he received. It had taken Elijah his entire ministry to build up to the point where he parted the Jordan River. It was the culmination of his life's work.

Now, the young prophet took his mentor's mantle and struck the water, imitating the methods of his master. When he did, the waters parted for him as they had for Elijah.

The *final* miracle of Elijah became the *first* miracle of

Elisha. Elijah's ceiling had become Elisha's floor. This wasn't an internal transaction that existed only in Elisha's mind. It was readily evident to anyone who observed Elisha's ability. As he crossed the Jordan again, the sons of the prophets who seemed to mock him earlier, were now waiting for him to return.

> *When the group of prophets from Jericho saw from a distance what happened, they exclaimed, "Elijah's spirit rests upon Elisha!" And they went to meet him and bowed to the ground before him.*
> **2 Kings 2:15 NLT**

Notice that although these men were also prophets, Elisha's hunger for impartation released a clear promotion that placed him on a higher level than his peers. They instantly recognized that the spirit of their former professor was now resting upon his understudy.

Later, we see that Elisha did take over his mentor's position within the school of prophets (2 Kings 4:38).

Impartation is a supernatural force that will take you higher in your calling than you could go on your own. Not only has God has given us an opportunity to advance in His kingdom, it's His expectation that we do.

A ROAD TO THE TOP

Anyone who has ever been dynamic in the kingdom of God has received multiple impartations. Your life should be no different.

No matter your gift or calling, there is already someone doing it at a much higher level. It is your responsibility to locate them and receive what they already have.

Elisha had access to Elijah. The disciples had access to Jesus. Timothy had access to the Apostle Paul.

I want to draw your attention to the fact that Elisha did not ask for a double portion of the Holy Spirit. Look closely at his request:

> *When they had crossed, Elijah said to Elisha, "Ask what I shall do for you, before I am taken from you." And Elisha said, "Please let there be a double portion of YOUR SPIRIT on me."*
> *2 Kings 2:9 ESV (Emphasis added)*

Elisha wanted a double portion of Elijah's spirit — and received it. Even the sons of the prophets recognized Elijah's spirit resting on Elisha.

It's important to note that you don't have to come into personal contact with the person from whom you want to receive impartation. You can hear someone teach or read what they've written and receive divine imparta-tion. That was the case for Ezekiel:

> *And as he spoke to me, the Spirit entered*
> *into me and set me on my feet . . .*
> *Ezekiel 2:2 ESV*

In fact, John the Baptist lived many years after Eli-jah had been taken into Heaven. Yet, the Bible says that John the Baptist came in the *spirit and power* of Elijah (Luke 1:17).

Timothy received the impartation of a spiritual gift from the Apostle Paul when Paul laid hands on him (2 Timothy 1:6).

You must locate those who stand in the area of your gift and calling and diligently seek their instruction, wisdom, and even a transfer of their spirit and power.

As you do, it allows you to leapfrog past where you really should be at your age and stage of purpose.

For example, Moses had spent much time gaining the trust and respect of the Israelites. They followed him as God's chosen deliverer who brought them out of Egypt.

However, when it was time for a transition in leader-ship, an impartation had to be released so that the same power to lead God's people would come upon Moses'

successor—Joshua. The likelihood that a crowd of almost three million people would transfer their loyalty
and allegiance to a younger, newly-appointed leader is
very slim. Without some kind of divine intervention,
there would definitely have been rifts and divisions
among the people, but look what the Scripture records:

> *Now Joshua son of Nun was full of the*
> *spirit of wisdom, for Moses had laid his*
> *hands on him. So the people of Israel*
> *obeyed him, doing just as the LORD had*
> *commanded Moses.*
>
> *Deuteronomy 34:9 NLT*

In the same way, when you receive impartation from
someone at a higher level, natural and spiritual things
respond differently to you. Just like Elisha, Joshua, John
the Baptist, and the disciples, you can operate in the
power of another (more advanced) person's spirit. That
is the power of supernatural impartation.

PRAISE IS A SUPERNATURAL
TRANSACTION THAT PROVOKES
GOD'S INTERACTION

#UnhangYourHarp

The Advantage of Personal Praise

I want to finish this book by giving you what I believe is the secret to lifelong success. It's the habit of personal praise. There is no substitute that can make up for the absence of personal praise.

I've shown you throughout the first part of this book how praise is connected to every blessing you receive from God. In this final chapter, I want to encourage you to make praise a personal habit. As you do, you will always have a reservoir of divine power that you can draw from on a daily basis. You will have an *advantage*.

David had an advantage that Goliath didn't know about. King Hezekiah had the same advantage even though the Assyrians weren't aware of it. Shadrach, Meshach, and Abednego not only had this invisible advantage that spared them from a torturous death, it changed their world as the King declared Jehovah to be the only God of their nation.

Praise is a supernatural transaction that provokes God's interaction. When God begins to interact with you, your advantage will clearly be seen.

PROMOTION BY
PERSONAL DEDICATION

I first began to consider this advantage of personal praise years ago after listening to an interview with worship leader and Grammy Award–winning recording artist Israel Houghton.

Houghton almost didn't exist. His mother became pregnant at the age of seventeen years old and was encouraged by her parents to have an abortion and move on with her life.

Although she decided to keep the baby, she was thousands of miles away from home, had recently split up with the father of her child, and the state of California was about to take her baby from her because she was considered an unfit mother as she was on drugs.

At the lowest point of her life, God sent a woman to encourage her.

"I don't know you, and I don't want to give you a hard time, but I was driving by and I really felt that I needed to come tell you Jesus loves you," the woman said. "You're not forgotten. It's going to be all right."

Because of that woman's faithfulness to share the gospel, Houghton's mother knelt down on the street outside of San Diego and gave her life to Jesus.

Years later, at the age of nineteen, Israel Houghton was playing the drums for a church in Phoenix, Arizona when they asked him to be the worship leader.

"I'll pray about that," he said mostly in an effort to deflect the offer.

"Pray hard," came the response, "because you start tonight!"

Israel was extremely inexperienced. By his own admission, he only knew three songs and they were all by Ron Kenoly. He sang them in every service for weeks until a woman in the church suggested that he go find who he was called to be in worship.

This sparked a hunger in Israel. He went home and grabbed his piano and pulled it into the kitchen. He figured that the tile floors would create better acoustics for singing and playing.

He would sit, play, and worship all by himself in the kitchen of his home. Four, five, and six hours would pass as he would sing to the Lord. He would sit there weeping and crying as he talked to God in times of personal praise and worship.

God began to interact with him and Israel Houghton's advantage became evident to all who were watching. He became the worship leader at Lakewood Church — one of the largest churches in the world.

He has won eleven Dove Awards, two Stellar Awards, six Grammy Awards along with eleven nominations, and produced twelve albums, two of which became gold records selling over 500,000 copies each.

Onlookers may assume that he is just a gifted musician or singer, but when you pull back the curtain on the life of any successful believer, you're sure to find a dedication to God's presence. That is the fuel for increase and never-ending success.

OUTWARD APPEARANCE MIRRORS INWARD PERSEVERANCE

Think of yourself as a container. Your ability to minister to others is a function of what's inside your reservoir. The Apostle Paul taught that although we are earthen vessels, we have a treasure hidden inside of our bodies. (See 2 Corinthians 4:7.) That treasure is God's power.

If we don't activate that power on a daily basis, it becomes evident that we are unfamiliar with the terrain. As I wrote in the section on habit two, tourists are experiencing something they're unfamiliar with, while tour guides are navigating others through terrain that they know like the back of their hand.

We should be able to easily navigate the presence of God because we've been there many times before.

I want to encourage you to schedule times of praise with God as you would with any other meeting on your calendar. One thing I've discovered after over thirty years of serving God is that if you don't prioritize spending time with Him, you never will.

Take out your phone, open the calendar app, add a new daily event, and choose a time that you won't be interrupted by distractions. Finish by setting a couple of alerts so that you can't miss it.

When the time comes, don't read the Word, pray, meditate, or listen to preaching or teaching. Spend that time praising God. Step into His presence and allow Him to fill your container with fresh oil from Heaven.

UNSHAKABLE

Your advantage makes you unshakable. Another wonderful way to say it is that you become *unstoppable*.

This is something David visualized at all times. He understood what his personal praise advantage afforded him. It was the source of his joy and peace:

> *I know the Lord is always with me. I will not be shaken, for he is right beside me. No wonder my heart is glad, and I rejoice. My body rests in safety.*
>
> *Psalm 16:8-9 NLT*

In the Old Testament, the unstoppable force of God's Spirit was right *next* to David. Things have changed. One of the wonderful benefits of our salvation is that we've become *new wineskins* capable of holding the new wine of the Holy Spirit. (See Matthew 9:17.)

In the New Testament, the Spirit of God isn't *next* to us; He is living *inside* of us.

> *The Spirit of God, who raised Jesus from the dead, lives in you. And just as God raised Christ Jesus from the dead, he will give life to your mortal bodies by this same Spirit living within you.*
>
> *Romans 8:11 NLT*

It's not enough to just be filled with the Spirit's presence and power. If we're truly going to be effective in our purpose for the Kingdom of God, we have to press our advantage.

If you're not familiar with the term *press your advantage*, it just means to use the dominant position you already have in order to succeed.

Continually praising God is the means whereby you can press your advantage. You're effectively leveraging your divine relationship in order to gain the benefits of *being* divine.

DIVINE RESULTS

In the story of Moses and the children of Israel crossing the Red Sea, we've always been taught that the water parted because Moses held up his staff.

Although he did hold up his staff as God instructed him, this is not why they sea parted for the Israelites.

Because Moses believed God, he obeyed God's instructions. There is no staff — including the one Moses held — that can part a body of water.

When Moses held his staff up, he was praising God. He was essentially saying, "We're stuck, Lord. There's nothing else we can do to succeed, but I believe you're more than able to make a way where there is no way."

Later, in the book of Psalms, we find out what really happened that day. Speaking of the Red Sea crossing the Psalmist wrote:

> *Your way was through the sea, your path through the great waters; yet your footprints were unseen.*
>
> *Psalm 77:19 ESV*

Notice it says *God's way* was through the sea. Although His footprints weren't seen by anyone, God was the first to walk through the Red Sea.

The water presented an obstacle to God's children obeying what He commanded them to do and where He commanded them to go.

God didn't free His people from slavery so they could spend the rest of their lives on the banks of the Red Sea. He gave them the Promised Land.

Because the water was hindering them from fulfilling His plan, it was in rebellion to Him. That's why the Scripture says,

> *When the waters saw you, they were afraid; indeed, the deep trembled.*
>
> *Psalm 77:16 ESV*

The reason the waters trembled when they saw God coming is the same reason Adam and Eve hid when God approached them.

Rebellion.

Although it looked impossible for God's children to escape, God opened a door that no one knew was there as He began to walk through the sea.

Which of God's creations are going to deny Him access? When He decides to move, who can stop Him?

> *The Lord of Heaven's Armies has spoken—who can change his plans? When his hand is raised, who can stop him?*
> *Isaiah 14:27 NLT*

Moses pressed his advantage by praising God and God gave him access to His actions. When we praise God, we have access to His thoughts and ways which are higher than our thoughts or ways (Isaiah 55:8-9).

Notice Isaiah wrote that when God decides to raise His hand, no one can stop Him from moving. I want you to see that praise is the element that moves the hand of God toward you.

You can take delivery of every blessing that God has set aside for your life by engaging Him in praise.

The Psalmist echoed Isaiah's words about the Almighty God. He described the outcome of people who understand the power that is found in the arm of the Lord. Look with me:

> *Your arm is endowed with power; your*
> *hand is strong, your right hand exalted.*
> *BLESSED ARE THOSE WHO HAVE*
> *LEARNED TO ACCLAIM YOU, who*
> *walk in the light of your presence, Lord.*
> *Psalm 89:13,15 NIV (Emphasis added)*

That's why the Lord inspired me to write this book. Praise is not a few fast songs before the slow ones. Praise is a supernatural key that moves the hand of God on your behalf.

PRIORITIZE YOUR FOUNDATIONAL PURPOSE

You have been created to praise God dynamically. It's important to understand that no matter what else we've been called to do, it never outranks our calling as a worshiper. You never graduate from the position of praise.

David praised God first. He continued to praise as a shepherd. He never became too tough to praise God as a warrior. He wasn't too dignified to praise God as a king. David never became too religious to praise God as a priest. Finally, he wasn't too reserved to praise God when he became a multi-billionaire.

Whatever your station in life, remember that praise is the element that positions you to go higher.

All God has ever wanted was our praise and worship. Not as beings who had no choice, but beings with a free will who would choose to praise Him.

That's why the *first* of the Ten Commandments is "You shall have no other gods before me." Additionally, in the New Covenant, our first commandment is to love the Lord with all of our heart, soul, and strength.

God wants all of your praise. I'll finish by giving you a verse that reveals God's desire and gives you access, as David had, to leverage the heart of the Almighty:

> *For you shall worship no other god, for the Lord, whose name is Jealous, is a jealous God.*
>
> *Exodus 34:14 ESV*

Acknowledgements

I continually thank the Lord for the spirit of wisdom and revelation that He releases to His people. I'll never take for granted the nature of God that is poured out to those who have become His sons. I'd also like to thank:

Carolyn. I love to watch you worship. Your passion for God's presence is inspirational to me and a wonderful model for our children to follow.

Madelyn, Brooklyn, and Teddy. My tribe of young worship warriors. Never stop praising.

Dad and Mom. Thank you for pushing me toward my gifts and talents and believing that I will always succeed.

R.W. Schambach Thank you for laying your hands on me and imparting the gift of God. I'll see you again in Heaven.

Chris Vance. Thank you for taking the time to sit down and show me so many things about praise and worship. Thanks for showing me how to play "Chris Vance chords" on the long-lost Korg N364. (You'll see that board again one day in Heaven. I've asked the Lord to fill your mansion with many of them.)

Lamce Palmer. Thank you for allowing me to spend time on the platform with you. I appreciate all the chord changes and charts you gave me. Thanks for being a great picture of what breakthrough praise looks like.

Brad Strobel, John Grimsley, & Tim Adams. You guys are the best at what you do. You're the best band someone could have and I appreciate all the time we've been able to praise together. Here's to many more years of successfully breaking through.

Megan Wiley. You ruined my guitar when I went away to Bible School. Please mail me a check for $599.

About The Author

TED SHUTTLESWORTH JR. is the founder of Miracle Word Ministries as well as Miracle Word University—an online Bible training school. He recently launched a digital network called Miracle Word Radio to broadcast the Word of God and strengthen the body of Christ. Ted has been preaching for close to two decades with a focus on winning the lost and showing the miracle power of God to a hungry generation. He is a graduate of Rhema Bible Training College and resides in Florida with his wife Carolyn, their two daughters Madelyn and Brooklyn, and their son Teddy III.

Prayer of Salvation

Heavenly Father,

Thank you for sending your Son, Jesus, to die for me. I believe that You raised Him from the dead and that He is coming back soon.

I'm asking you to forgive me of my sin and make me brand new. Give me holy desires to pray and read your Word. Empower me by Your Holy Spirit to live for You for the rest of my life.

You are the Lord of my life. I thank you that the old life is gone and a new life has begun, in Jesus Name, Amen.

....

If you prayed this prayer, please contact us. We would like to send you a free gift, pray for you, and help you take your next steps in Christ.

info@miracleword.com

DIVINE PROTECTION BELONGS TO YOU
BECAUSE OF YOUR COVENANT WITH GOD

It seems fear has intensified in America and around the world. Whether it's viral outbreaks of disease, the economic downturn of 2008, breaking news about groups like al-Qaeda and ISIS, school shootings, or attacks like we saw in Paris and Brussels, the hearts of people seem to be filled with terror.

Should Christians be worried as the days grow darker before the coming of the Lord? Is there hope and protection for God's people? I believe there is. This book will reveal how you can access the protective power of God Almighty, while the workbook will take you into a deeper study of your biblical covenant.

AVAILABLE NOW AT SHOP.MIRACLEWORD.COM

YOU MAY HAVE THE FASTEST CAR IN THE WORLD
BUT IF THE GAS TANK IS EMPTY IT'S NOT GOING ANYWHERE

In *Praise. Laugh. Repeat.*, Ted Shuttlesworth Jr. challenges you to discover the power of the overwhelming joy of the Holy Spirit. The Bible tells us that the joy of the Lord is our strength. If the enemy is able to steal your joy he has also stolen your strength and the momentum to do what you've been called to do. You can shed the skin of depression and enter into feather-light living for Jesus Christ beginning today!

The *Praise. Laugh. Repeat. 40-Day Devotional* is specifically designed to be a primer that sets you on a path to the overwhelming joy of Heaven. The amount of spiritual strength you wield is directly connected to the amount of God's Word you've received into your heart.

AVAILABLE NOW AT SHOP.MIRACLEWORD.COM

MMX **MIRACLE WORD** VII

IN KNOWLEDGE. BUILD YOUR FAITH. HARASS THE DEVIL.

at if you could receive anointed Bible School training without even having to get off your
ch? Now you can! *Introducing Miracle Word University*, an online training resource deed to give you an understanding of Pentecostal and Charismatic doctrine at a very af-
able price—only $69 per course!

cover subjects like the Holy Spirit, divine healing,
hecy, tithing and giving, how we got our Bible,
many more!

GET STARTED TODAY AT
MIRACLEWORDU.COM

WATCH OUR VIDEOS ON YOUTUBE

DOWNLOAD OUR FREE APP

CONNECT WITH SOCIAL MEDIA

 /MiracleWordMinistries

 Ted Shuttlesworth Jr.

 @tshuttlesworth

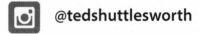 @tedshuttlesworth